healing through play

Using the Oaklander Model

Part 2: More Treasures

A Guidebook for Therapists and Counselors
Working with Children, Adolescents and Families

By
Karen Fried, PsD. LMFT
Christine McKenna, LMFT, LPCC
May 2025

Edited by Alisa Reich
Book Design by Shelly Short
Cover Illustration by Fabio Magnasciutti
Graphics by Kathy Miu

ISBN#: 979-8-218-83229-2

Karen Fried, Psy.D., M.F.T. is a licensed Marriage and Family Therapist and an Educational Therapist and consultant in Los Angeles, California. She has a private practice in Psychotherapy. Karen uses the Oaklander Model of Child Therapy in her practice and is the immediate past President of the Violet Solomon Oaklander Foundation. She trains child and adolescent therapists and educators in the US and internationally. Training, online tools, and many resources can be found at https://www.karenfried.com.

Chris McKenna is a Licensed Marriage and Family Therapist and Licensed Professional Clinical Counselor in Santa Monica, California. She currently works in her private psychotherapy practice and has many decades of experience working in school settings as a teacher and counselor. She is a VSOF Board Member and a certified Oaklander Model Trainer and Supervisor.
https://www.chrismckennatherapy.com

Chris McKenna and Karen Fried

Table of Contents

- 11   INTRODUCTION
- 19   KIND WORDS
- 25   VIOLET'S CORRESPONDENCE
- 31   GETTING STARTED WITH THE OAKLANDER MODEL
- 39   KEY CONCEPTS
- 47   THE PROJECTIVE PROCESS
- 51   PROJECTIVE EXPERIENCES
- 61   STRENGTHENING THE SENSE OF SELF
- 81   SELF-NURTURING PROCESS
- 87   PARENT EDUCATION AND FAMILY WORK
- 97   WORKING WITH ADOLESCENTS
- 101   PLAY THERAPY IN GROUPS
- 109   SCHOOL COUNSELING
- 117   TELEHEALTH TREATMENT
- 131   TERMINATION
- 137   HIDDEN TREASURES
- 169   MORE TREASURES

Forward

In 1995, Chris McKenna, Karen Fried, and Sue Talley met at Violet Oaklander's summer intensive trainings in Santa Barbara, California, which drew therapists from around the world. They all met Lynn Stadler shortly thereafter. We knew learning Violet's playful and powerful approach straight from her was pretty wonderful, both personally and professionally-so much so that Karen and Sue asked Violet if they might meet with her monthly for supervision. Happily, Violet agreed. Those monthly meetings soon included lunch, which Lynn joined. They would continue to the end of Violet's life, and built deep friendships.

When Violet retired from training, Sue suggested we create the Violet Solomon Oaklander Foundation (VSOF) to continue her work. Lynn, Sue, and Karen began training in the Oaklander Model in Malibu, California, usually joined by Chris, with help from Sue's sons, Blake Brisbois and Max Greenberg. Violet's family also helped establish and administer VSOF. Her grandson, Siri (the son of Mha Atma and daughter-in-law Martha), lent his technical skills for the website, conferences, and myriad details. Daughter Sara Oaklander gathered Violet's publications and promoted the VSOF board's efforts. Violet's daughter-in-law Martha Oaklander culled and summarized her handouts, case files, meticulously saved correspondence, and notes for trainings she led at prestigious American and international institutions of learning. As a consequence, readers of this guidebook will see quotes from these undated, unpublished pieces ascribed to Violet but without any formal cite information. Readers will also notice Violet's rejection-way before her time-of the default use of masculine pronouns (he, him, his) for therapist and client, and her conscientious alternating of feminine ones (she, her, hers) with these. We continue her inclusive practice by using gender-free plural pronouns (they, them, their/s) regardless of classic rules of grammatical agreement. Also in accord with her respect for each client, we secured permission to share all drawings, photographs, and statements presented in this book and removed any identifying information from them.

Many others aided us as well. Claire Mercurio, also a founding member of VSOF, who graciously served as treasurer for many years, produced a documentary of Violet's life, *Making Lemonade*. And, based on over 10 years of participating in Violet's trainings, Peter Mortola wrote and published his University of California at Santa Barbara doctoral dissertation as *Windowframes*, now translated into 7 languages and consulted worldwide. Currently presided over by Karen, VSOF board members Camille

Jarmie Harris, Mha Atma Khalsa, Chris McKenna, Claire Mercurio, Peter Mortola, Lynn Stadler, and Patric White dedicate countless hours to disseminating Violet's contributions.

In 2020 Chris, Karen, Kathy Miu and Shelley Short composed the first guidebook for the many trainees who had requested a way to access Violet's theory and experience. Shelley's expert management let us employ those participants as focus groups to help devise the title, layout and wording of *Healing Through Play using the Oaklander Model: A Guidebook for Therapists and Counselors Working with Children, Adolescents and Families*. Thankfully, we were able to show Violet the guidebook draft and receive her comments. We were so grateful that she went through every page, providing heartfelt and wise edits. Now in 4 languages with more translations planned, the guidebook has been used by therapists, counselors, and teachers throughout the US and internationally. Yet COVID-19 and crises throughout the world soon made new therapeutic guidelines-and thus a new edition of our guidebook-crucial for healing professionals.

During the pandemic Karen wrote "Just for Now: Using the Oaklander Model in a Crisis," and, unable to deliver it live, decided to present her work-and Violet herself-on a Zoom call. With that technology and the renown of Violet's model through her *Windows to Our Children* and *Hidden Treasure*, the call reached practitioners and educators in 6 countries. Continuing to this day, ensuing Zoom calls draw hundreds of therapeutic professionals from 35 countries. So what began as a one-time call letting Violet greet therapists across the planet (most waving their well-worn copies of *Windows*) evolved into an ongoing global forum for her (until her passing in 2021) and for them to learn from other practitioners of her model (Fried, Psychotherapie-Wissenschaft, Vol. 13 No. 1 [2023], https://psychotherapie-wissenschaft.info/article/view/1664-9583-2023-1-59). Many of these experts have adopted and expanded Violet's model in their practice of treating children and in training other child therapy experts, and have become close colleagues and friends. After Violet's death, we honored her on a Zoom call attended by over 100 people, from longtime colleagues to those who had met her on the "Just for Now" calls.

Most important, the Zoom calls both sparked requests and supplied opportunities for online Oaklander Model training and treatment. A global necessity during the pandemic (and, sadly, a few wars) and a lasting gain in access to care, telehealth platforms transformed therapeutic teaching and practice. Kathy Miu developed the online sand tray tool (onlinesandtray.com), which let therapists use play therapy interventions with children and families via telehealth, and which continues to serve 20,000 users per month in as many as 114 countries. Next, Karen, with expert technical help from Mike

Jones, Jake Zohdi and Hannah Hwong, released the online dollhouse (onlinedollhouses.com), online puppets (onlinepuppets.org) and, most recently, the mindful draw (mindfuldraw.com) and mind-body applications. All these apps can be found on playtherapyapps.com and are entirely cost-free to care providers, students, and clients. Equally important, telehealth researchers have found these tools' efficacy equivalent to that of their in-person originals (Fried, https://psychotherapie-wissenschaft.info/article/view/1664-9583-2023-1-59).

This second edition of the *Healing Through Play* guidebook is meant to be an additional companion to the Oaklander Model Trainings, along with Violet's books, Peter Mortola's, and our first guidebook. This 2nd guidebook introduces the treasures from Violet's files we reviewed after her passing in 2021 and also includes the telehealth options Karen developed during the pandemic. Just as Violet's *Hidden Treasure* detailed the theory underlying *Windows to Our Children*, our second guidebook provides more Oaklander Model theory and interventions to enable play therapists to design diverse, individualized treatment plans.

Certainly, we regret not having Violet's feedback on this version, but look forward to receiving yours. We hope we have done her work justice and that it supports you in your therapy with children, adolescents, and families.

Chris and Karen

Violet Oaklander

Introduction

This guidebook is divided into chapters that provide:
- Key concepts explained
- The therapeutic process outlined for therapists to get started using the Oaklander Model
- The theory and use of the projective process
- How to use this model to strengthen a client's sense of self
- Understanding why, how, and when to use the self-nurturing process
- Termination process covered
- Application of the Oaklander Model to working with:
  – Parents
  – Schools
  – Adolescents
  – Groups
- Review of the use of play therapy apps for Gestalt Play Therapy via telehealth
- More interventions for treatment planning in chapters *Hidden Treasures* and *More Treasures* at the end of this guidebook.

The Therapeutic Power of Play

Play offers the child the opportunity to learn about his world and try out his world. For the child play is serious, purposeful business through which he develops mentally, physically, and socially. Play is the child's form of self-therapy, through which confusions, anxieties and conflicts are often worked through. Through the safety of play every child can try out his own new ways of being, be it gentle, aggressive, thoughtful or tough. Play performs a vital function for the child. It is far more than just the frivolous, lighthearted, pleasurable activity that adults usually make of it. Play also serves as a language for the child—a symbolism that substitutes for words. The child experiences much in life he finds difficult to express in language, and so he uses play to formulate and assimilate what he experiences. Play encourages the use of the imagination in many forms. It encourages a freedom and expansion of the spirit, a letting go of inhibitions and restrictions. Play is essential for the child's healthy development.

The therapist who works with children can make use of this powerful tool in her therapeutic work with children. She provides a milieu and materials that are conducive to helping the child work through aspects of his life that cause difficulty. Further, it is essential that the therapist, herself, be a willing and experienced player.

In the Gestalt Therapy context, play refers to all of the activities and experiences the child and therapist engage in within the therapeutic setting.

Wisdom of the Child and Role of the Therapist

Even very young children have a wisdom about themselves that is awe-inspiring. The therapist's task is to assist the child in sharing this wisdom. As the therapist gently opens the doors to self-awareness and self-ownership, it is through such open and contactful sharing that the child strengthens his or her own self.

Gestalt Therapy with children can be directive and at times non-directive. The therapist makes a treatment plan based upon the therapeutic needs of the child and suggests experiences to meet treatment goals. However, she is sensitive to the child's desires and energy. **In fact, the therapy session is like a dance: sometimes the therapist leads and sometimes the child leads.** Many children come into the session knowing exactly what they want to do. Others perseverate on an activity and require a slight "push" to attempt something new. Often the therapist will negotiate with the child, dividing the time between both. In any case, the therapist is interactive with the child, rarely sitting back and merely observing the child's play.

Remembering the various ages of one's own childhood—remembering what it is like to be a child—is the therapist's greatest tool. Sometimes asking oneself, "What would I like to hear right now if I were the age of this child" can reap great rewards. **Children are complicated and fascinating and it is a privilege to have the opportunity to do this work.**

Gestalt Therapy in Child Development

Violet viewed Gestalt Therapy as effective for child therapy, both in assessment and treatment. Rooted in Fritz Perls's emphasis on the "here and now," Gestalt Play Therapy prioritizes experience over insight. Violet said, "Experience is more important than awareness." She defined play in this therapeutic context as "all of the activities and experiences the child and therapist engage in within the therapeutic setting," emphasizing its role in emotional expression and healing. Play encourages imagination and "a freedom and expansion of the spirit, a letting go of inhibitions and restrictions." Rather than providing interpretations, therapists can use "tentative translations, guesses, and hunches that the child can verify," ensuring children feel truly heard and understood.

Integration and Growth

Gestalt Play Therapy can help children integrate all aspects of themselves, develop self-regulation, and build a strong sense of self. Violet often said, "This enables children to release blocked or negative emotions that can lead to inappropriate behaviors…. It allows children to find more appropriate coping behaviors…[and] monitor their reactions." By focusing on the "what and how" of behavior rather than the "why," children gain awareness of their actions and can make meaningful changes.

Children Are More Than Their Behavior

Violet believed that "each child is a unique, valuable human being" who, when given the right opportunities, can engage with the world as "an integrated, aware, responsible, dynamic, creative person." She emphasized that "children already know how to grow, how to develop, how to learn, how to expand and discover, how to feel, laugh and cry and get mad," and that all they need—just like the child within us—is the opportunity to do so. She felt, "Children are not their behavior…. Children raise their voice when they are not heard."

In early 2012 Charles Schaefer, editor of many works on play therapy, asked Violet to list the top 10 things every play therapist should know. Ever-generous Violet offered 11:

11 Things Every Play Therapist Should Know

1. Play is the child's way of communicating.
2. Establishing a relationship with the child is a prerequisite to everything else.
3. It's OK to have fun.
4. The child often knows what he or she needs to do, and sometimes the therapist needs to lead.
5. It's important to have a variety of materials to encourage expression, such as clay, paper, pastels, paints, puppets, musical instruments.
6. Many symptoms that bring children into therapy have as their underlying cause withheld and suppressed anger. Various forms of play using encounter bats, drums, mallets for pounding clay, etc., can help the therapist encourage the child to gradually express this anger in a fun and playful way.
7. The contact between the therapist and child needs to be evaluated at all times. If the child breaks contact, something else is going on that the therapist needs to be aware of.
8. The therapist has the responsibility to stay in contact with the child.
9. The therapist needs to use a normal voice when talking to the child. The child is very sensitive to a patronizing voice.
10. The "play" taking place between the child and therapist is the child's therapeutic work.
11. It is important to pay attention to the child's body language, evidence of [emotional] restriction, and so forth.

"Violetisms"

Nothing happens without the relationship.

Children raise their voice when they are not heard.

Play is the child's way of communicating.

In fact, the therapy session is like a dance: sometimes the therapist leads and sometimes the child leads.

Experience is more important than awareness.

Children are not their behavior.

Resistance is the child's ally.

Anger is the most misunderstood and least tolerated emotion.

Children already know how to grow, develop, learn, expand and discover, feel, laugh, cry, and get mad.

See the inner realms of the child through fantasy.

I don't fix kids.

Top 10 Things Play Therapists Must Know to Design Individualized Treatment Plans

Violet saw that the flexibility of Gestalt Play Therapy and its celebration of personal agency allow therapists to tailor treatment to the individual child: "The Gestalt therapist is ever cognizant of the wider potential of each child to grow and develop in healthy ways. It is the task of the therapist to guide the child toward her rightful path of growth…[as] the child innately knows how to grow and develop." In an email of March 30, 2012, Charles Schaefer asked Violet and other practitioners for the top 10 things a play therapist needs to know about a child to formulate an individualized treatment plan. Violet responded:

1. How well does the child relate to others: parents, siblings, teachers, other children? Does she relate easily to the therapist?
2. Can she sustain contact appropriately with her parents, teachers, other children? Books? Toys?
3. When did the behavior that brought her into therapy begin? What was happening in the family at that time?
4. Has there been some trauma in the child's life? (abuse, loss, hospitalization, divorce, etc.)
5. How does the child express anger? (How do the family members in general express angry feelings?)
6. Does the child appear to have a poor sense of her own self? (Does she appear to be overly attached to her parents or others?)
7. What are the child's symptoms: physical (as stomach aches)? Is she overly anxious? Show signs of OCD? Phobias? Bed wetter? Encopretic?
8. What is my experience with the child? How does she present herself to me? Does this differ from reports from parents? Others?
9. Does the child's body appear restricted?
10. What is the family dynamic?

Kind Words

Thank you all for your kind words. Karen and Chris

I am eagerly awaiting the release of the second book by Dr. Karen Fried and Christine McKenna, which is a real guide and invaluable support in studying the nuances of working with children and adolescents according to the Oaklander model. This guide describes the best techniques used in the therapeutic process. It helps the psychologist to comprehend the intricacies of working with parents, the importance of working with aggressive energy and self-nurturing processes. It also highlights key aspects of working with children and teens in today's fast-changing and technology-driven world. Without a doubt, this work is a vital key that will help practicing psychologists unlock the secrets of working with children through the Oaklander Model.

~Bulatevych Nataliya,

PhD, Associate Professor of Developmental Psychology Department,

Taras Shevchenko National University of Kyiv, Ukraine

We hear it all the time, "our children need more play in their lives," and this is true now more than ever. This is why I am so eager for Chris and Karen's Second Guidebook. We clinicians need to refresh, reboot, and be reminded of what matters, and to return to the tools that help us grow our work. When working with their material, I always feel reconnected to the community of child therapists they bring together, allowing the material to come alive. I will be pre-ordering my copy as soon as possible!

~Lauren Curnyn LMFT

I've been waiting for this book. The first volume has stayed within arm's reach in my private practice for years. This one builds on it beautifully, offering even more ways to bring the Oaklander Model into a wide range of therapy spaces.

Karen and Chris write in a way that feels deeply human and immediately useful. From projective work to telehealth and groups, the content is practical, thoughtful, and ready to use. One of the reasons I love learning from them is that you can almost hear Violet's voice in the background, with their clinical wisdom and experience woven through every page like a violet ribbon...respectful, revealing, and restorative.

If you work with kids or teens, keep this book and their *Healing Through Play* guide close. You'll reach for them again and again.

~Jackie Flynn, Registered Play Therapist Supervisor and EMDR Consultant, Author of *EMDR with Kids Flip Chart*

As a clinician who has worked in both private practice and school settings, I have found the Oaklander model to be a powerful tool for helping children and teens explore their inner world, heal, and access their creativity. This second book thoughtfully expands on Violet's legacy, offering both new and seasoned practitioners an experiential framework that is deeply meaningful and effective in connecting with young clients.

~Daisy Gómez, Psy.D.

I live and practice in Sri Lanka, and it feels very alone and far away from the Oaklander community, so Karen and Chris's new book is a precious resource for me, and I can't wait to have it in my hands! The simplicity and effectiveness of their writing style makes this an invaluable addition to any therapist's library and I am truly grateful for their effort.

~Seema Omar, Counselor

Chris McKenna and Karen Fried's workbook "Healing Through Play Using the Oaklander Model" should be in every child and family therapists' library. I use their techniques often with my clients to decrease stress levels and process traumatic events. Their approach makes psychotherapy engaging, fun, and transformative.

~Justine Roach, LCSW

A garden of stories from around the world. Make contact with the paths we have taken to become therapists.

~Laura Saldarriaga, Licensed therapist, Colombia

I am Sheila Shrestha from Nepal, and Healing Through Play Using the Oaklander Model is one of my favourite books on our school's counseling resource list. I have been using the activities from this book with my students in both individual sessions and group settings, and it has made a real difference in how they express themselves and grow emotionally. This essential guide seamlessly blends the Gestalt approach with dynamic play techniques to offer powerful interventions. The second volume dives even deeper to foster authentic connections, strengthening the sense of self, and nurturing emotional growth. It provides practical tools and strategies for building I/ Thou relationships across various contexts, from individual and group sessions to family work and school counseling.

Whether you are a therapist, counselor, or educator committed to supporting children's social-emotional well-being, this book is a treasure trove inspired by the profound work of Violet Oaklander.

~Sheila Shrestha, Gestalt therapist, Nepal

Healing Through Play Using the Oaklander Model: Volume Two is an essential companion for all child therapists seeking to deepen their practice with creative, relational, and developmentally attuned tools. Karen Fried and Chris McKenna, gifted clinicians and master trainers mentored by Violet Oaklander herself, offer a rich, expansive guide that honors Violet's legacy while meeting the needs of today's therapeutic world.

From strengthening a child's sense of self to engaging in powerful projective and self-nurturing processes, this book provides accessible and meaningful interventions across modalities and settings—including school counseling, group work, telehealth, and family therapy. It thoughtfully addresses topics often overlooked in child therapy, such as countertransference, termination, and working with adolescents.

Whether you are new to the Oaklander Model or a seasoned practitioner, this volume is filled with practical gems—from session forms to unpublished insights—that will deepen your connection to clients and expand your therapeutic impact. It is a privilege to learn from Karen and Chris, whose heartfelt and skilled guidance brings this healing work to life. This book is not just a resource—it's a treasure trove for any therapist working with children, teens, and families.

~Tammi Van Hollander, LCSW, RPT-S™, RST-C/T

The legacy of Dr. Violet Oaklander comes to life in a practical and tangible way in this remarkable guidebook. In this second volume, Karen and Chris build upon Violet's pioneering work with deep appreciation and the wisdom of their own experience.

With clarity and creativity, they translate Violet's teachings—and even share unpublished treasures—into tools that are accessible and highly relevant in today's therapeutic landscape.

This guidebook feels like a heartfelt tribute to Violet's life's work. Karen and Chris honor her approach and invite us to meet children where they are—with presence, respect, and playfulness—just as Violet taught us.

~ Liz Cervantes MS QMHP-R

Exploring the upcoming second volume of Healing Through Play feels like being lovingly handed the heart of Violet's work—again, but with even more creativity, clarity, and generosity. Karen and Chris have crafted a guide that stays true to the essence of the Oaklander Model while making it accessible to people from diverse backgrounds and clinical realities. That's exactly what this model is about. It's the kind of book that becomes a staple—one you return to again and again for inspiration, guidance, and grounding in the work we do with children and families.

~Michelle Urrutia Williams, Clinical Psychologist & Certified Oaklander Model Trainer

Violet's Correspondence

We found so much correspondence to and from Violet in her files. We have included some of it here for your enjoyment.

12-10-1985

Dear Violet Oaklander Ph.D.,

I really want to thank you for responding to my letter, I was so excited I phoned my mother long distance just to tell her that I got a letter from Violet Oaklander. My mother was excited because I was excited as a result we were two excited people on the phone.

8-11-1982

…I'm especially fascinated by the technique of asking the child to BE one or another of the objects in his/her drawing and to speak as that object. The therapeutic possibilities of this technique are, to me, vast and rich and exciting especially when you take it a step further by asking the child if he/she ever, in real life, feels the feelings expressed the object in the art work. Aside from the obvious immediate therapeutic benefits of such an approach, it seems to me that a child being treated in this way is also being encouraged to develop a sensitivity to metaphor, symbol and imagery which will surely increase his/her creativity and artistic expression in the years to come.

11-19-1982

…This is the second time I have heard you speak but have been using your book as a "Bible" in my private practice.

10-19-2019

…I have been disheartened when I see adults who do not respect of value the feelings of children.

…This is just a short note to say, "thank you!" I think this book is simply genius. It is inspiring me each day both in my personal and professional life.

Despite all the fan mail, Violet's responses reveal a true humility. Her correspondents and students often heard her call her advice on working with children as "obvious." Commenting on her iconic Windows to our Children, she ascribed its publication to its unique on-the-ground utility rather than any particular excellence:

From correspondence with Nancy Oppenheim, Eastern Institute for Gestalt Therapy student

June 25, 1977

"…I don't have a publisher yet but I'm positive the book will be published since there really isn't anything available like this. There are millions of books on working with children but pretty much they don't actually tell you exactly how to work with kids in a therapeutic situation. From the letters I have already received from various parts of the country and the response I get from the classes I teach and the workshops and seminars I do, I know there's a tremendous need for this kind of a book and I hope my contribution will be helpful."

After the book's enthusiastic reception, Nancy Oppenheim's responded:

"Violet—we think you were right! The work has become the bible of projective therapy with children and families, allowing youngsters not only to flourish as self-aware selves but honing their grasp of metaphor, symbol and imagery, which increases their creativity, artistic expression, and comprehension of others."

Always the generous teacher, Violet answered hundreds of inquiries from all over the world, as she did for a Ukrainian therapist who asked,

"How to become a good child psychotherapist? What should I do? What is the most important thing?"

3-5-2018

Dear ____,

I just came across your email and I noticed that I didn't finish answering your question about how to be a good psychotherapist for children. Please forgive me; I'm 91 and things slip by me. To be a good therapist one must really like children and be able to remember what it was like to be a child. Having some experience with children would be helpful. Other than that you need to make your own way.

Good luck with your work.

Warm regards,

Violet

Violet Oaklander's works and their translations attest to the universality and continuity of her therapeutic approach.

Our first *Healing Through Play* was translated into 3 languages, allowing therapists from many countries to understand and apply Violet's ideas and experiential interventions easily and comprehensively.

Peter Mortola's widely translated *Windowframes* shows readers how Violet conducted her training and led experiences, in her own words.

Getting Started

Getting Started Forms can be accessed with this QR code. You may use any of these forms individually or order the packet online.

Scan QR Code to Download

https://karenfried.squarespace.com/intake-packet

Getting Started Oaklander Model

Here's what's in the Getting Started with the Oaklander Model Packet:

- **Child/Adolescent Intake Form:** Please note this is a template Karen designed to record information and consent statements for practices in the U.S; feel free to modify this for your use.
- **Assessment Form and Worksheet:** The Assessment Form contains 12 questions to clarify the level of the child's contact functions and sense of self. The Assessment Worksheet lets you note how your client appears and behaves when beginning treatment.
- **Contact Forms:** Let you interview the child about each of their senses, so you can gauge how contactful they are with each.
- **Contact Functions Awareness Chart:** Used in an interview, this form clarifies, for the client and therapist, the client's awareness of their contact functions. Make the interview a fun, engaging (thus effective) activity by putting out the sensory items: things to touch, such as sensory discs with varied textures; things to see, such as kaleidoscopes, magnifying glasses; things to hear, such as musical instruments; things to smell, such as fragranced pens or herbs; and if appropriate for the setting, things to taste (if eating is not allowed in the setting, talk about favorite and least favorite foods with the client). The information from this interview can be used with other intake information to fill out the next form, the "Goal Setting Card."
- **Goal Setting Card:** Use it with the client to identify and set goals for the items on the Assessment Form at the child's various settings.
- **Treatment:** This form can be used in many ways. You can interview the client, and/or turn each one into a projective experience with drawings, projective cards, sand tray scenes and other projective interventions.
- **Timeline:** This template asks the child to mark the events of their lives, or a short period of time, in chronological order.
- **Sense of Self: Making Choices; Likes/Dislikes:** This form strengthens a child's sense of self by allowing them to affirm what they like and don't like as well as affirming parts of themselves. The form also provides the opportunity to explore their negative feelings about aspects of their life--an expression that is often discouraged. The choices presented here are common, and most children have opinions on them. But feel free to design your own based upon your creativity and the needs of your clients.

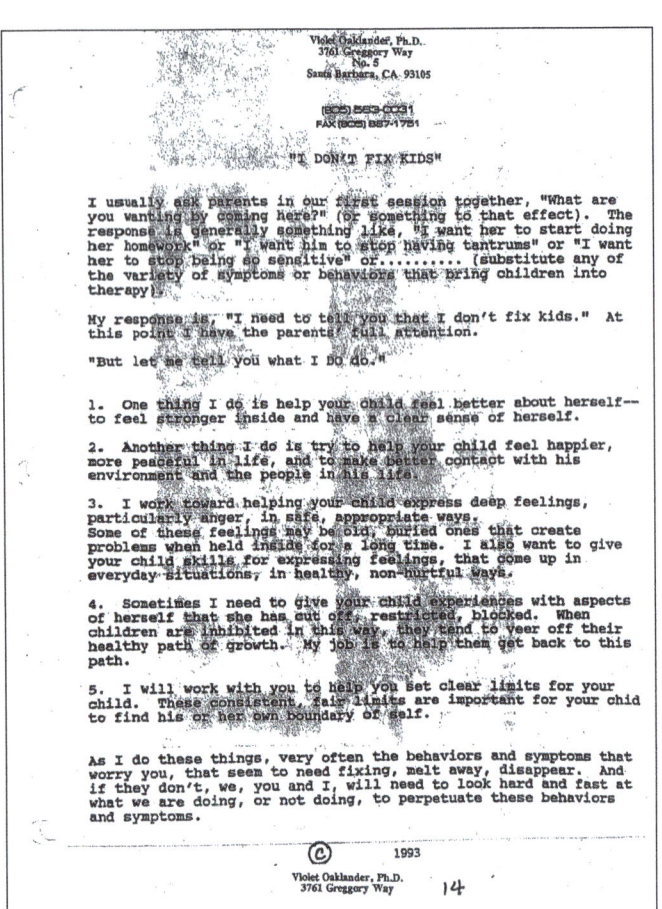

I Don't Fix Kids

Violet conveyed her approach to the family with her handout stating that therapy isn't about the child needing "fixing" of some pathology or brokenness. "I Don't Fix Kids" set the stage for an I-Thou relationship, with its basis of mutual respect and genuine connection. Once she grabbed clients' attention with this handout, Violet specified what does happen in the therapeutic process and how that can help children.

You'll find Karen's Session Forms and Getting Started - Oaklander Packet on page 32 that can be accessed with a QR Code. The forms cover intake; assessment; setting therapeutic goals; interventions; setting up your play therapy room; and presenting a case. You may use any of these forms individually or order the packet online using the QR code.

- **Sense of Self Series:**
  - **"I Am" Worksheet:** Karen designed this form in our Sense of Self series based on Violet's teaching that when a client makes self-statements, they are strengthening their sense of self.
  - **Perceptions from Self and Others:** This allows the child to imagine and express their sense of their own inner and outer selves. The form can be adapted to any child by using age-appropriate vocabulary.
  - **Polarities:** Since polarities (characteristics of the self that are the opposites of acknowledged qualities) are at play in most issues in our lives, this form facilitates their recognition and integration. Children, especially teenagers, Violet writes in *Hidden Treasure* (2006, p. 111), are "plagued by polarities." So it's helpful and relieving for them to understand different sides of themselves to gain perspective on issues they're facing.
  - **Past Present Future:** This form develops the client's perspective on what they have experienced, lets them reflect on the present (a core focus of here-and-now Gestalt Therapy), and encourages them to express their desires and worries about the future.
  - **Body and Movement:** Facilitating contact with the body, this form can be used in many ways, including its prompts. It offers the games Simon Says and Pantomime as options, but the same prompts may be employed in creative dramatics, puppets, drawing and other activities.
- Incomplete Sentence Form: This form can be used to facilitate the client's expression of thoughts and feelings with a prompt to guide them, which reduces pressure and frees them to communicate about sensitive or complex issues.
  - **Coat of Arms:** This exercise helps clients explore and express their personal identity, values, strengths, and important life experiences symbolically. Clients select and draw images or elements that represent various aspects of themselves in response to prompts.
- **Setting Up Your Play Therapy Room:** Karen devised a list of items we recommend for your work with children and teens. It's not necessary to have every item; the most important component is your playful, genuine presence.
- **Sense of Self Rating Chart:** This form lets you assess your client's sense of self. It's helpful to share this with caregivers as appropriate and, depending on the age, the client. We recommend using the form at the beginning of therapy, and revisiting it when you are measuring progress.

It's also useful when determining and documenting the appropriateness of termination.
- **Presenting a Case:** As supervision is extremely valuable in clinical work, we recommend completing this form before meeting with your supervisor or consulting colleague.

Graphic by Kathy Miu. Copyright Healing Connections by Karen Fried

Initial Contact:
- Begins with parent/caregiver sharing concerns.
- Therapist provides information about approach, experience, availability, and fees.
- For your information: Please see customizable intake forms found on **page 32** to obtain background information.

First Session:
- Child and caregiver attend together.
- Discussion about the child happens in their presence to build trust.
- Exceptions may be made based on clinical judgment.
- Main goal: Build rapport and set the stage for a second session.
- Review procedures, gather information, and explain confidentiality in clear, age-appropriate terms.

Ongoing Sessions:

- Child typically attends 4–6 individual sessions.
- About every 6th session, meet with child and caregiver to:
  - Share observations.
  - Review progress.
  - Plan next steps.
- Additional check-ins as needed.

Relationship

Violet emphasized the importance of the I-Thou relationship, based on Martin Buber's philosophy, as the foundation of the therapeutic alliance. A non-hierarchical, respectful connection fosters safety and healing. While, as seen in the graphic on the left, the therapist may have more age, education, and experience, their role is to be an equal participant in the therapeutic process—not a superior or authority figure.

Ways to establish the I-Thou relationship in the very first session

- Include the child with the parent/s whenever possible.
  - That way the child is present when the therapist hears what is being said about them.
- Ask the child questions to show that you the therapist cares about the child's point of view. Even if they respond, "I don't know," the child can still be seen and heard beginning with the first session.

"Do you know why you're here?"

"What are your goals?"

"What's one thing you'd like to share that you think is important for me to know?"

"What would you like to do during our session?"

Please note:

- Honor any resistance that comes up.
- Follow the child's energy and contact.
  - They don't have to "finish" an activity or "own" its meaning. Allow them to be "done" whenever they say they're done.
  - Recall that felt experience is more important than conscious awareness.

Getting Started

Key Concepts

Definition of Terms and Description of their Role in Gestalt Play Therapy

In this chapter we define central terms in the Oaklander Model of Gestalt Play Therapy, and explain how these **key concepts** function in work with children, adolescents and families.

Gestalt Therapy: Experiential, client-led therapy based on a mutually respectful, specific, and genuine "I-Thou" therapist-client relationship

Contact:

Contact signifies the ability to be fully present, "with all the aspects of the organism vital and available." Healthy contact activates the senses (looking, listening, touching, tasting, smelling); the ability to express emotions (wants, needs and feelings); the use of the body; and intellect (learning, expressing thoughts, being curious). When any of these modalities are inhibited, restricted or blocked, good contact suffers. Fragmentation, rather than integration, occurs and the child's sense of self is compromised; "Children who have troubles, who are grieving, worried, anxious, frightened or angry, will armor and restrict themselves, pull themselves in, inhibit themselves, and block...expression. Healthy contact involves a feeling of security with oneself...."

Emotions:

Contact with emotions allows for children to gain awareness of and express that part of themselves. Emotional literacy includes understanding what emotions are; their unique manner of experiencing them; and ways to express them through creative and projective modalities.

Sense of Self: includes awareness and contact with the 5 senses, taste, hearing, sight, smell and touch. Awareness of one's body, breath, and voice. A sense of self is strengthened when a child/teen develops a sense of mastery, has the ability to make choices, has appropriate power and control, can define themselves using self-statements, may be able to own projections and all while using playfulness, imagination and humor.

The Senses and **the Body:**

Contact with the five senses and the body strengthens the sense of self. Violet taught that when children restrict their thoughts and feelings, their sense of self becomes diminished. The therapist's role is to help the child strengthen their contact functions (using senses and movement; feeling; thinking) through creative activities like art, storytelling, and play.

Projection:

By using projection as a therapeutic tool, Oaklander helped children bridge the gap between their internal experiences and external reality, empowering them to express themselves and heal. It lets them externalize and reveal and express what has been hidden from their awareness. Such indirect, metaphoric productions like drawings, clay work, or sand tray scenes can allow them to recognize and sometimes own the projected aspects of themselves. Violet stressed that even without their owning the projection, and without the therapist's interpretation, the client benefits from the experience.

Contact-Boundary Disturbances: Confluence, introjection, deflection and retroflection

Early trauma can affect the child's ability to be in contact with themselves and to be aware of a boundary between themselves and others. As Violet explained, "Ideally, children perceive contact between parts of themselves and between themselves and others. Disturbances occur when they experience harm from the environment. Since they are not yet capable of setting their own boundaries, harmful external contact [can cause] internal disturbance [and] diminish their sense of self." These disturbances may manifest as *confluence, introjection, deflection,* and *retroflection.*

Confluence: Over-identification with another

An overly compliant child who only agrees with no sign of resistance to others "indicates that this child's self is so fragile that she must do whatever she is told…in order to feel that she can survive." In her Mind/Supermind online talk, Violet compared a child's development to "merging, as when two rivers join." Initially feeling one with the mother, the child soon struggles to separate and establish independence. "This struggle is a major developmental task for children and continues through adolescence, with brief moments of equilibrium." Even adults face ongoing challenges in defining themselves. As Violet noted, "The child is already beginning to shape and form her very being as she paradoxically struggles to separate and find her own self while avoiding rejection, abandonment, or disapproval. This is not an easy task."

Introjection:

Young children often misinterpret or internalize those messages from the environment about themselves without being able to evaluate their validity. These introjects from early childhood can influence behaviors and resurface later if not addressed.

Beliefs and **Behaviors**:

Violet said, "Every one of us has some faulty beliefs about ourselves which leads to behaviors we hate, but can't seem to change. Actually we are all operating on the belief system of a four- or five-year-old little

Key Concepts

Polarities Drawing:

"Standing in Flowers Enjoying Myself/Not Like My Life Where I have to work a Lot"

person…. What we believed then about ourselves and how we chose to be in the world is what we still believe and do now."

Egocentricity:

The child, especially in the earliest years, is cognitively and emotionally unable to understand external, separate experiences. Thus they feel responsible for any positive and negative events in their lives.

Deflection:

Children and adolescents use deflection to avoid dealing directly with material and emotions they find too difficult or painful.

Retroflection:

Children retroflect as a coping mechanism when they can't deal directly with an issue. For example, they may retroflect the emotion of grief by turning it inward, and experience physical symptoms such as stomachaches or headaches.

Polarities:

Children and adolescents benefit from gaining experience with and awareness of the polarities that exist within them. They may be overly aware of one part, like their negative qualities, which are often the reasons they are in therapy. By addressing the polarity, the client becomes aware of more aspects of themselves.

Emotional Expression:

As Violet stated, "As the child feels more support within herself, she is able to move toward emotional expression…[through a] variety of creative, expressive, projective techniques." Anger, often the most challenging emotion for children, may be suppressed or misdirected. "Attention is given to this important expression which causes so many problems." Using drawings, dramatics, clay, puppets, and other techniques, children learn to normalize and process anger, from mild annoyance to rage. "Focusing and working through these feelings to achieve a peaceful, calm state of being is part of the healing process," making emotional regulation a key therapeutic goal.

Expressive Techniques:

These techniques include a variety of experiences and materials such as creative arts, play, sand tray, puppets, music, dramatics, sensory and body awareness, storytelling and using imagery, fantasy and metaphor. The process of employing them is powerful, enjoyable, and applicable to all developmental levels and in individual, group and family settings.

Resistance:

Violet often said, "Resistance is the child's ally; It is the way she takes care of herself. I expect resistance and I respect that resistance. I am more often surprised when it is not there, than when it is." Gestalt Play Therapy honors resistance, inviting an experiential projective expression of it rather than criticizing or analyzing it, as a way of meeting the client where they are.

For some children—especially those with early emotional injuries—forming a relationship takes time. In these cases, the relationship itself becomes the therapy. Throughout, Violet stresses the importance of respecting resistance as a form of self-protection and finding creative, non-threatening ways to connect.

Awareness and Experience:

While awareness is important in therapy, for young children especially, Violet prioritizes experience over awareness. Experiences such as projective exercises can be therapeutic without having to achieve the client's conscious awareness or, in Oaklander terms, "own the projection." For her, "all of these experiences serve to strengthen the child's self, promote good contact functioning, culminating in healing emotional expression, and…facilitate new, more satisfying ways of being in the world."

Mastery:

Children have a developmental need for the experience of mastery, as Violet notes ("The Therapeutic Process With Children and Adolescents," *Gestalt Review* 1(4), p. 299): "Children who live in dysfunctional families…often grow up too fast and skip over many important mastery experiences vital to healthy development. In some cases the parents may do too much for the child, thereby thwarting his need to struggle; other parents are so rigid they don't allow the child to explore and experiment. Some parents believe that frustration improves staying power. Children *never* learn to accomplish tasks through frustration. There is a fine line between struggle and frustration, and it is important to be sensitive to that point. The baby struggles to put the smaller box into the larger one, but when frustration sets in he begins to cry. The older child loses energy—cuts off contact."

Self-Regulation:

Children of any age seek homeostasis, which is a constant re-balancing in response to stressful events. A strong sense of self allows children to self-regulate when stressed. Inappropriate or disproportionate reactions are signs that children are attempting, however unsuccessfully, to regulate themselves.

Self-Nurturing Work:

Violet said, "Children take in many negative messages about themselves, particularly in early childhood. These…introjects (as noted above) are fragmenting, that is, they cause children to split off. A part of the child will feel stupid, for example, while another part might be angry about this feeling. The self-nurturing process assists children to deal with these negative messages in order to achieve integration. They are helped, through a variety of creative exercises, to contact and strengthen that nurturing aspect within the self to help them become more accepting, caring, and actively nurturing to themselves."

Transference, Countertransference:

While Violet acknowledged that transference can enter the therapeutic relationship, her model does not use it in the therapeutic process: "Transference generally enters into any relationship, however I do not encourage it. The child may react to me as a parent figure; however, I am not her parent. I have my own point of view … limits and boundaries.… I am not hopelessly enmeshed with her.… As I maintain my own integrity as a separate person, I give the client the opportunity to experience more of her own self.… I have a responsibility to be aware of any 'buttons' pressed in me that may not be genuine emotional responses to the contextual situation, and to explore these countertransference responses to eliminate their detriment to the client.… I honor what's important to me.…" (HT, p.21)

She guided therapists to acknowledge, and address, countertransference so they could focus on the current relationship with their client.

Unfinished Business:

Past situations that have not been resolved—unfinished business—can result in what appears to be an overreaction to current events.

The Projective Process

EXPRESSIVE, PROJECTIVE TECHNIQUES as fantasy, art, clay, storytelling, puppets, sand tray work, music, creative dramatics, therapeutic metaphors, games.

WHY? 1. Most are powerful projections --children do not come in to say "This is what I want to work on." HOW we use these is significant, and when I show you some slides, you will see.

2. The way people have expressed themselves for thousands of years. These techniques cross language and cultural boundaries. And physical handicaps.

3. They are fun --children learn to enjoy, laugh--an important aspect of the self.

4. Some of these techniques define boundaries and build the self, as well as help them express those buried emotions.

5. They help children experience new ways of living.

EXPERIENCE IS THE KEY HERE. Children benefit mostly from therapeutic experience, rather than awareness.

What if children are not willing or able to use these techniques?

RELATIONSHIP

CONTACT

Basic to the therapeutic process.

Violet's Original Handout

Theory, Use, and Challenges

Theory

Violet's theory of using projections is a key idea in her work: when children engage with something outside themselves—like a drawing, story, or movement—they often express parts of their inner world. Creative activities are natural ways for children to explore and express themselves. This section outlines the projective process and the steps used in projective activities, along with examples.

This handout shows that projections can be used with any media.
- Why? Projective activities are used because children don't say, "This is what I want to work on."
- People have used projective activities for thousands of years and these techniques cross language, cultural and physical boundaries.
- They are fun.
- Allow for new ways of expressing themselves, their emotions and have a new experience in their lives.
- Experience is more important than awareness.

Use

Violet's basic procedure is simple, flexibly open to follow-up questions as appropriate, and highlights what the therapist should observe.

Projective Experiences

Sequence of Dr. Oaklander's Work

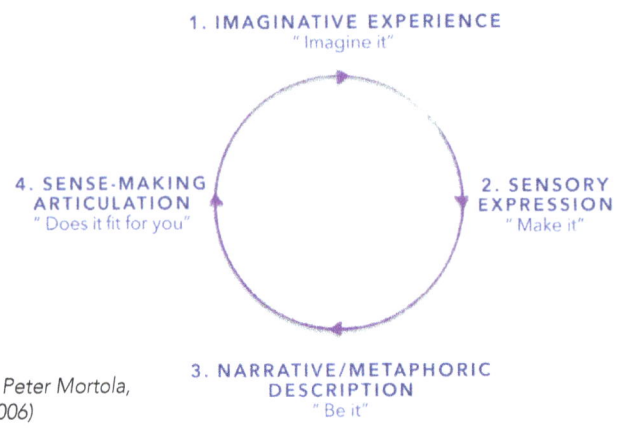

Adapted from Dr. Peter Mortola, Windowframes (2006)

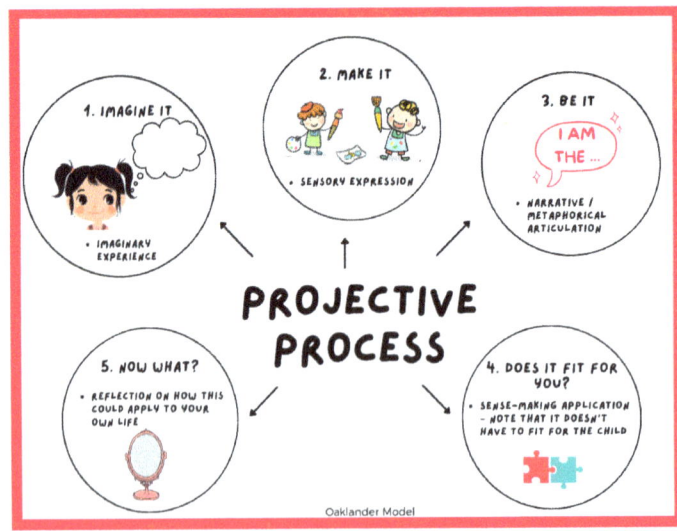

Copyright Healing Connections by Karen Fried

Processing the Projection

Violet's "Notes to Myself" affirms that her approach can apply to most issues children face:

"Re specific topics as child abuse, divorce, loss and grief, etc.: It's actually the same work. It's a matter of assessing where the child has cut off the self, and then giving experiences to strengthen and regain the self, particularly the expression of blocked feelings. Also, it is important to know the common issues involved and how children are affected by them."

Violet explained the process of doing projective activities with clients in the handout shown in the previous chapter. **Please note that according to Violet, if a child does not go through all of these steps, it is OK - any of these steps are still therapeutic for the child. Peter Mortola and then Karen consolidated these steps in the graphics of 4 and then an additional 5th step process.**

1. Clients are first asked to Imagine a scene.
2. They then are asked to make the scene, using any projective media: sandtray, clay, drawing, puppet stage, etc. This step enables:
   – Expression of the self
   – Affirming one's identity
3. Then clients are asked to share the experience of making the scene:
   – their feelings while drawing or making the sand tray, etc.
   – their process

Therapists can then observe their process: Did they rush, go slowly, get frustrated, make contact with you?

4. Clients are then asked to describe the scene (sand tray, clay object, etc.) in their own way.
5. Clients are then asked to elaborate on the scene:
   – Make the parts clearer and more obvious.
6. Clients are then asked to be parts of the scene:
   – Describe the shapes, forms, colors, objects and people.
   – Ask the client to "be" a part of the picture. Then ask the client to describe the picture using "I am the…."
   – As needed, provide details: "Be the _____ and describe yourself; what you look like, what your function is (etc.)."
   – Watch for missing parts or spaces. As appropriate, invite the client to "be" the empty part or space.
7. There is a chance to deepen the work. Clients can be asked:
   – Focus attention by emphasis and exaggeration of a part of the picture. "What is it like to be the _____?"
   – Ask questions. "What do you do as the _____?"
   – Encourage dialogue between two parts. "What would the _____ say to the _____?"

Projective Experiences

8. Observe the client to measure contact, withdrawal and possible resistance.
    - Watch for cues in voice tone, body posture, facial expression, breathing, silence.
    - Silence can mean censoring, thinking, remembering, repression, anxiety, fear, or awareness of something.
9. The client is then given the opportunity to own the projection:
    - "Does this fit in your life in any way?"
    - "Do you ever feel that way?"
    - "Could you say that for you?"

    The client may say, "No."
    - Maybe resistance and/or still-weak sense of self.
    - Even without owning, clients benefit from the experience: All steps are therapeutic.
10. So now what? Based upon the insights gained from the experience, the client can talk about how they can apply this to their life,
    - "If appropriate, leave the scene and move onto life situations."

Violet Oaklander, Ph.D.
3761 Greggory Way
No. 5
Santa Barbara, CA 93105

USING PROJECTIVE TECHNIQUES ©

Therapeutic Steps:

1. Being willing to do the projective activity, as drawing, clay, puppets, sand tray, storytelling.

2. Telling about their drawing-to the therapist or someone else. Telling about how it felt to do it or about how they went about doing it. Sharing the experience of doing it. Talking about it.

3. Entering into the metaphor, the image. Becoming a part of the picture--being the object, the puppet, etc. Elaborating, giving details. Seeing the situation from the perspedtive of the object or part of the whole. Which one is you? Describe yourself. Dialoguing with object. What's going on--what's happening. The story comes out.

4. Owning the projection. This can be done at two levels.

    A. Symbolic level: Child can tell about the situation, but only at the level of the metaphor. Fragmentation continues within the personality.

    B. Reality/personal level: Child connects that what is exerienced within the matephor is also experienced in her life. This deepens the work and allows what has been difficult to share, or has been out of awareness, to come into awareness. "Do you feel that way? Does that fit in your life in any way? etc." Can move into other work from that.

5. Throughout this process watch for resisitance. When it emerges, respect it. Also watch the child's body and evidence of affect.

Assessment is important: a confluent child may say yes to everything. Or the child may not understand what we're asking. We may be off the mark. The child may not have enough support to own anything.

Watch for patterns, themes, polarities, stuck places.

Example: Toy exercise--Choose a toy. Look over your toy. Become the toy. How would you describe your object without naming it. What's it like to be you? (tree, animal, boat, etc.) Projection takes place as we move away from the object from our sensory experience (touching, seeing) into language, and more and more into the story.

Violet's Original Handout

Resistance:
- A sign of highly significant material to be explored and processed.
- Intuitive, visceral knowledge of what she can and cannot handle and I trust the process.
- A manifestation of energy and of the contact level.
- Visible before the child's own awareness: by observing his body response I may say "Let's stop this for now and play a game" to the great relief of the child (obvious through the body).
- Passively demonstrated; ignore, act distracted, seem to not hear, or do something other than what I have suggested.

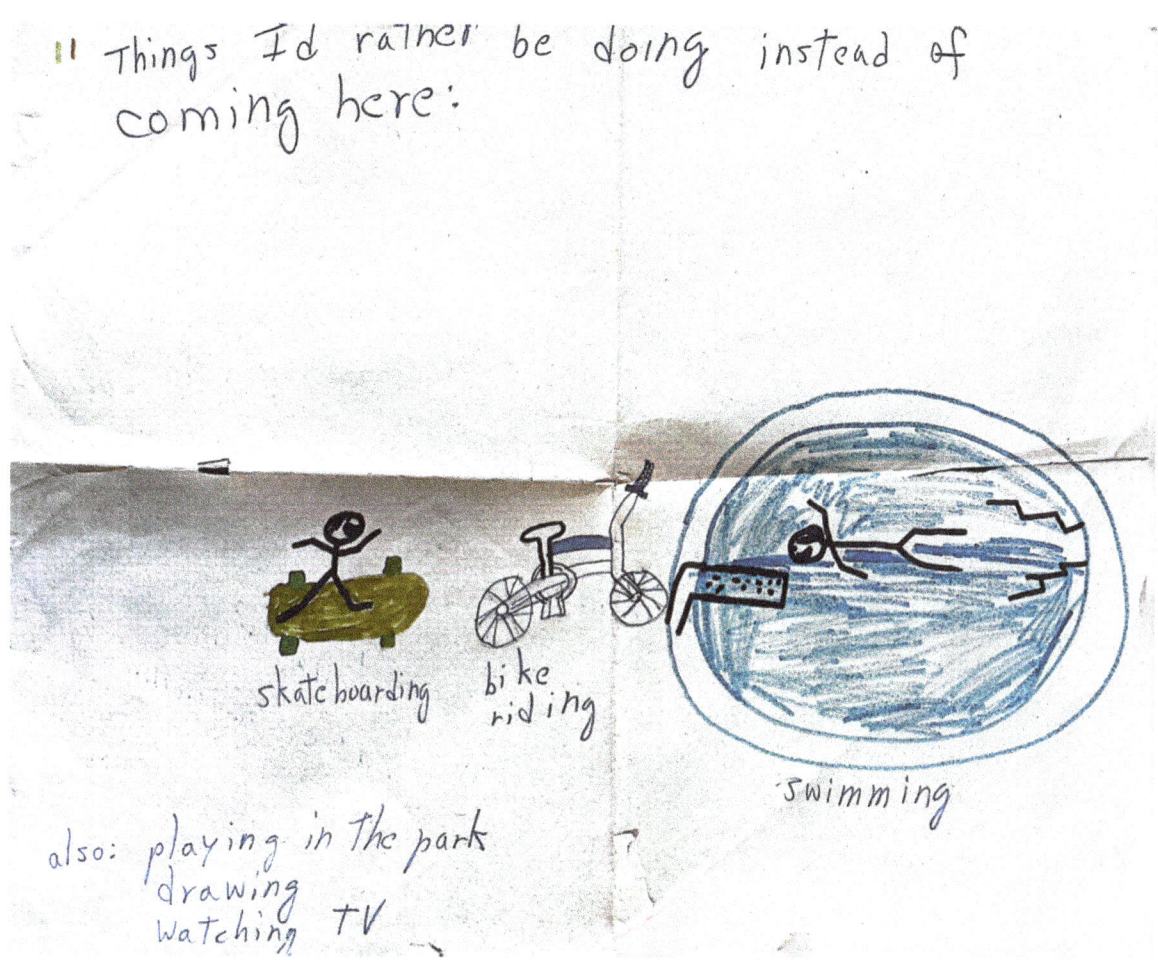

"Things I'd rather be doing instead of coming here:

Similarly, whether or not a client is aware, or "owns" what they've projected their experience still has therapeutic value. In fact, Violet found the experience alone—even without conscious grasp of its meaning—to be healing.

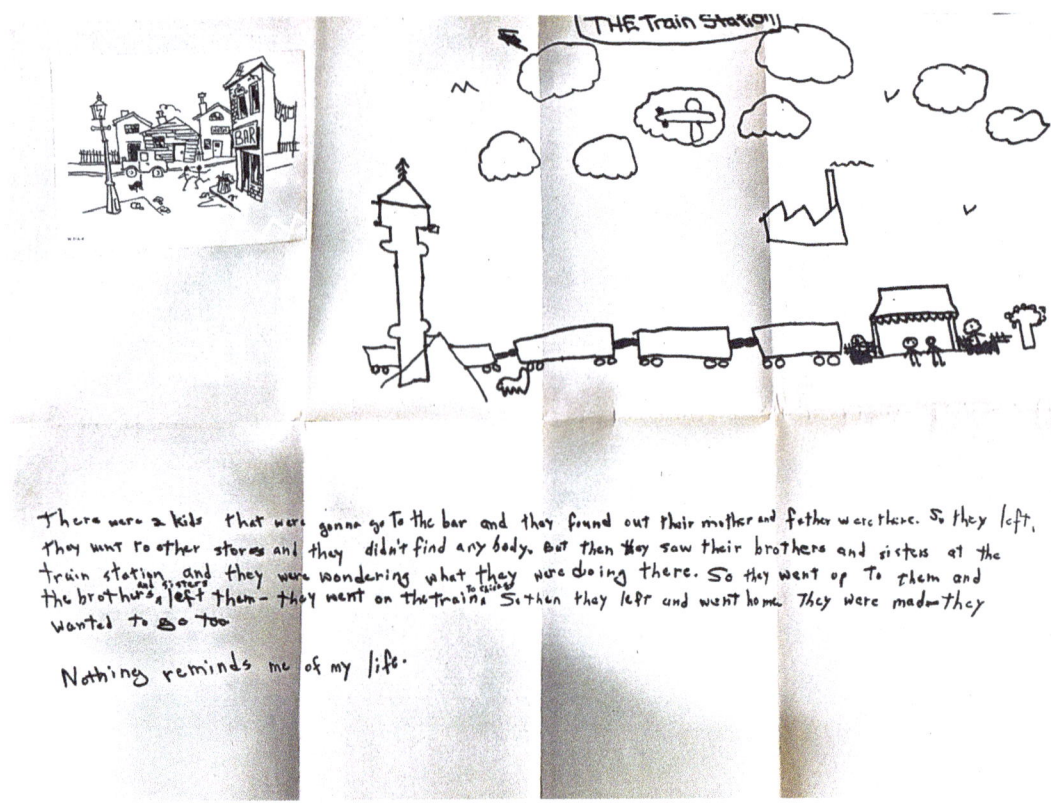

An example from Violet's files of not owning a projection: The client is not yet owning the projection but is clearly talking about themself.

(Text: There were 2 kids that were gonna go to the bar and they found out that their mother and father were there. So they left. They went to other stores and they didn't find anybody. But then they saw their brothers and sisters at the train station and they were wondering what they were doing there. So they went up to them and the brothers and sisters left them - They went on the train to Chicago. So then they left and went home. They were mad they wanted to go. Nothing reminds me of my life.")

Example of Not Owning a Projection: The client is not yet owning the projection but is clearly talking about themself.

Violet devised many interventions to help clients feel comfortable creating and owning projected expressions. But she assured therapists that, as long as they honor their clients' readiness, the activities will strengthen their sense of self by activating their contact with and expression of that self.

Awareness and Experience

Awareness allows anyone to be conscious of the aspects of their lives. The experiences in the Oaklander Model can promote awareness(es) which might include sensations, feelings, wants, needs, thoughts and actions. "As the child moves through the therapy experience, he becomes more aware of who he is, what he feels, what he needs, what he wants" (Oaklander, 1982). Some older children as well as adolescents can often become aware of unsatisfactory ways of being, experience them fully with the guidance of the therapist, and begin to experiment with conscious choices for new behaviors. This is often, Violet says, beyond the scope of younger children. For these children, experience is the key to their therapeutic process. These experiences may be with aspects of themselves that are blocked such as one or more of their sensory modalities. All of these experiences serve to strengthen the child's self, promote good contact functioning, culminating in healing emotional expression, and, in general, facilitate new, more satisfying ways of being in the world. Often, after such therapeutic experiences, the unacceptable, worrisome behaviors drop away."

Strengthening the Sense of Self

We might all agree that helping a child develop a strong sense of self is an important goal of therapy. And then the question that logically follows is, "how?" This graphic below illustrates how.

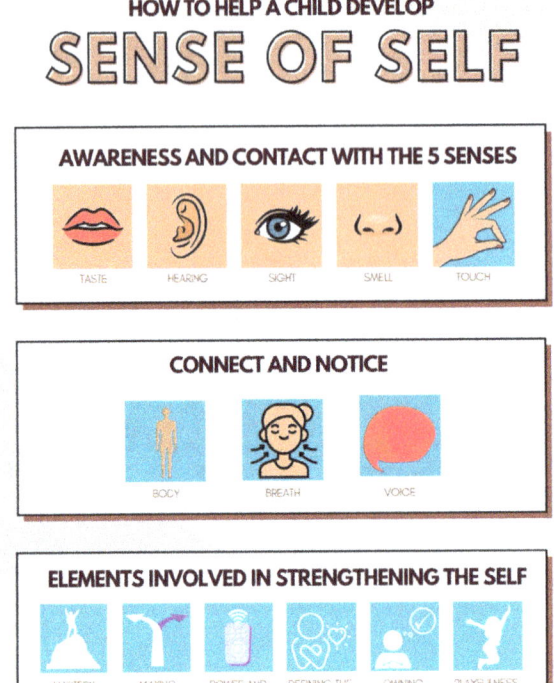

Graphic by Kathy Miu
Copyright Healing Connections by Karen Fried

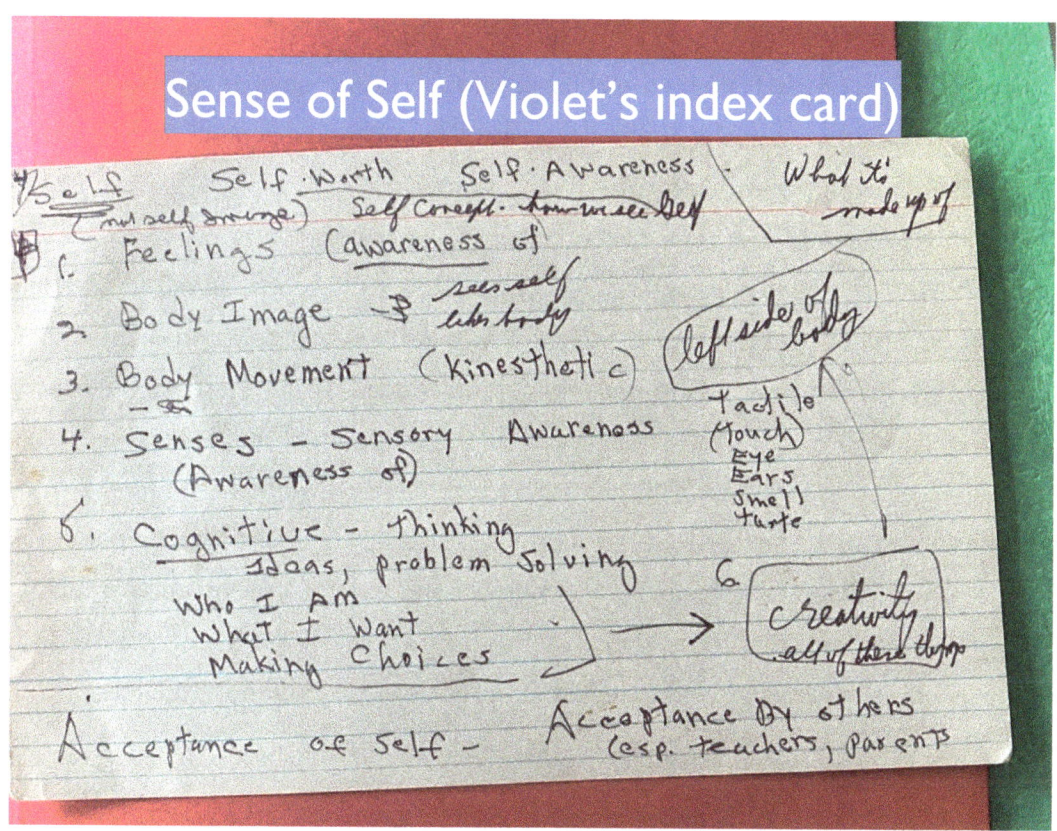

We were going through the many many many :) files of Violet's notes, cases, drawings, etc. and stuffed into a folder was this index card. We were so awed by what we read from Violet's scribbled notes. On this card we felt, is the essence of her model: how the self is formed and supported. Here was to borrow from her some true "hidden treasure." We outline below how each concept can be part of the therapeutic process.

Violet often said that, "nothing happens without a relationship." Therefore, we preface activities to correspond to this treasured index card with a strategy to establish the I/Thou relationship - mirroring.

Strengthening the Sense of Self

Senses and the Body

We found in Violet's notes: Helping the child develop a strong sense of self is a prelude to emotional expression, an important step in the healing process. When children restrict and inhibit aspects of the organism, the self is diminished. Strengthening contact skills play an important part in this process. These skills, which we sometimes refer to as the functions of contact, are looking, listening, smelling, tasting, touching, moving in the environment, expressing thoughts, ideas, opinions, and defining the self. Strengthening these skills give the support necessary for expressing deep emotions that block healthy functioning and integration. A variety of experiences introduced by the therapist are used to strengthen the child's self which in turn provide the self-support required for emotional expression. This is not a linear process—the therapist presents these activities as needed. In Gestalt work with children, experience plays a vital role in strengthening the self. The therapist provides a variety of activities to help the child experience aspects of the self: defining the self, feeling some power and control, making choices, achieving mastery, owing parts of the self through projections in stories, art, activities, etc. being playful and imaginative, contacting his inner, energetic strength, and abiding by clear boundaries and limits. It is through these experiences that the child begins to feel a stronger sense of himself.

Violet's index card transcribed

Self	Self-Worth	Self-Awareness	What it's made up of

- Feelings: awareness of
- Body image: sees self, likes body
- Body movement: kinesthetic
- Senses: Sensory Awareness- touch, eyes, ears, smell, taste
- Cognitive: thinking, ideas, problem solving
- Creativity: Who am I, What I want, Making choices

Acceptance of self, Acceptance by others, especially parents and teachers

Graphic by Kathy Miu. Copyright Healing Connections by Karen Fried.

Interventions for Feelings:

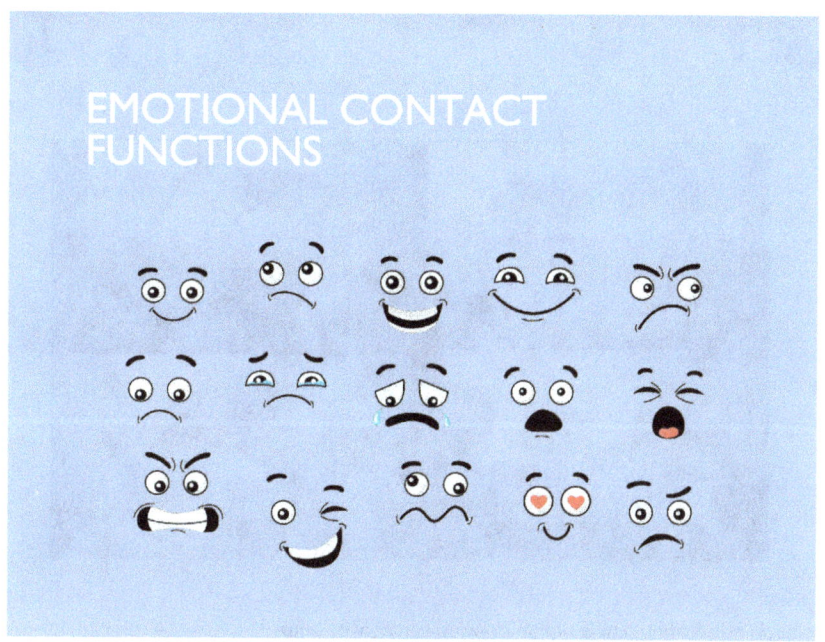

*Graphic by Kathy Miu showing different feelings.
Copyright Healing Connections by Karen Fried.*

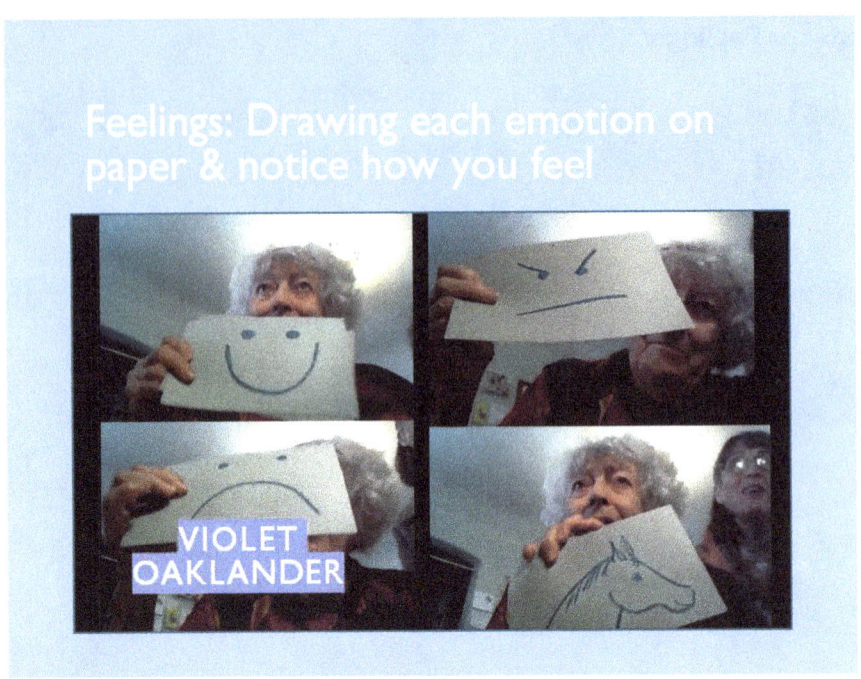

Violet demonstrating how a simple drawing can convey emotions. Source: Just For Now online meeting.

As the sense of self becomes stronger, the child or adolescent can better experience, recognize, tolerate, and reflect on blocked feelings/emotions. We can:

Create a Safe and Supportive Environment
- Establish an I-Thou relationship
- Set up a safe, inclusive therapeutic space (office or virtual)
- Use varied arts techniques (drawing, painting, sculpting, storytelling)
- Support Identification and expression of Feelings

From Violet's Files

Strengthening the Sense of Self

From Violet's Files

Interventions include:
- Write a letter
- Draw a picture

Identify triggers - see More Treasures for the Emotions List - Things that Make Me…

- Empty chair
- Puppet shows
- Collage
- Sandtray
- Family sessions discussing feelings
- Unfinished business

Increasing Awareness of Emotions-Body Link

Promote awareness of how emotions manifest in their body. Help clients identify physical sensations associated with different emotions (e.g., a racing heart accompanying anxiety). If appropriate, note the neurophysiological connection between emotion and the body.

Working with Anger

Violet wrote in her article, "The Many Faces of Anger," that anger is "undoubtedly the most difficult emotion for children to deal with. Often children appear angry, but the authentic anger is not expressed. Other children mightily suppress any anger energy … which causes so many problems."

She designed many interventions to express and allow the client to manage anger. First, "All the various aspects of anger, from mild annoyance to rage, are introduced through drawings, creative dramatics, clay, puppets and other projective techniques," exercises which "assist the child in normalizing her angry feelings." Then, the treatment moves to "focusing and working through these feelings to achieve a peaceful, calm state of being." That healing step of "learning how to deal with everyday anger is an important part of the therapeutic process."

Violet wrote about adolescents and anger: "The more an adolescent shows anger in a session, the easier it is to establish a working connection, because they trust the therapist with their strongest emotion. In fact, if an adolescent is "cold" angry, little can happen until the anger is brought into the open and acknowledged."

Adolescent Anger

- They don't suddenly become angry: When their needs haven't been met, behavior accelerates as they seek homeostasis. This results in fragmentation and a thicker armor of self-protection:

- Age-appropriate development of independence may cause them to withdraw from family.
- They often experience shame, despair, fear of the future, grief, fragile sense of self and fear of losing more of self, all of which can appear as a "bad attitude" or moodiness.
- Increasing cultural demands weigh on them and should be considered.

Interventions for Anger: Guidelines

- Don't interpret the anger. Don't tell them what they're thinking or feeling.
- Use simple questions: "How do you feel about coming here?" or "It seems like you don't want to talk. How come?"
- Silence is ok.
- Firmness is ok.
- Be honest regarding confidentiality ahead of time.

Defining sources of anger and rating their intensity can help children/teens learn about their emotions from a cognitive perspective:

Anger Triggers

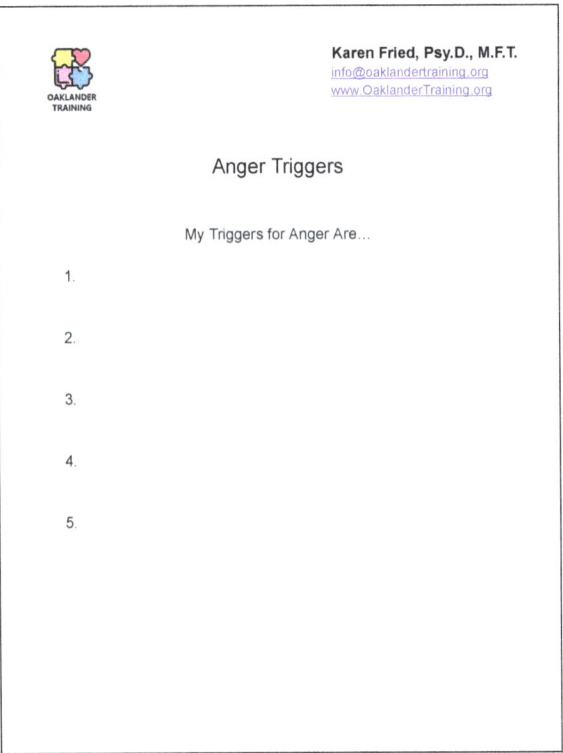

Anger Triggers Tool

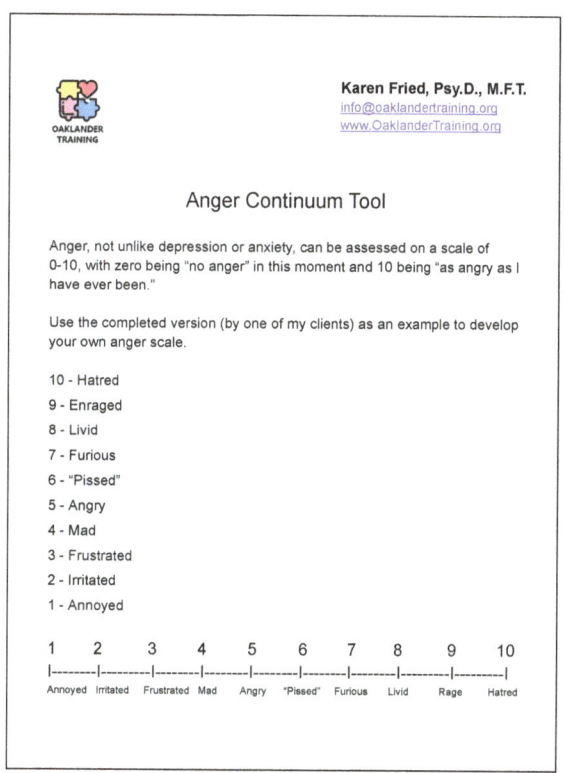

Anger Continuum Tool

- Anger Collage or Anger Sand Tray
- Clay: Invite the client to make something that represents their anger, and then, if they'd like to smash or tear it.
- Books to Read Together or Stories You Read Aloud: Discuss angry characters.
- Anger Collage or Anger Sand Tray
- Clay: Invite the client to make something that represents their anger, and then, if they'd like to smash or tear it.
- Empty Chair: The client can imagine and then talk to, the source of their angry feelings present in the chair(s).
- Writing: The client can write an angry letter or a list of things they don't like about their family, school, friend, or other.
- Family Session: Discuss anger. Have each family member pick an item that represents each of the other members. Each person says, "One thing I like about you is_____. One thing I don't like about you is _____."
- Distinguish Unfinished anger from Resolved Anger: Ask, "How do you know it's unfinished?"

Strengthening the Sense of Self

(There are still feelings and/or triggers around that issue/event/person.) Ask, "How do you know you've worked through it?" (There's a calm and regulated feeling associated with that issue/event/person.)

Interventions for the Body: Body Image

The Oaklander Model addresses body image and self-esteem issues. Clients are encouraged to explore their perceptions of their bodies and any self-worth judgments tied to body image.

"How I think I look," "How I wish I looked," and "How I think others see me" are all sample prompts to address body image issues.

From Violet's Files

From Violet's Files

With the Somatic Drawing, the child can draw what they are feeling in their body to address any somatic issues.

Gabe's headache:

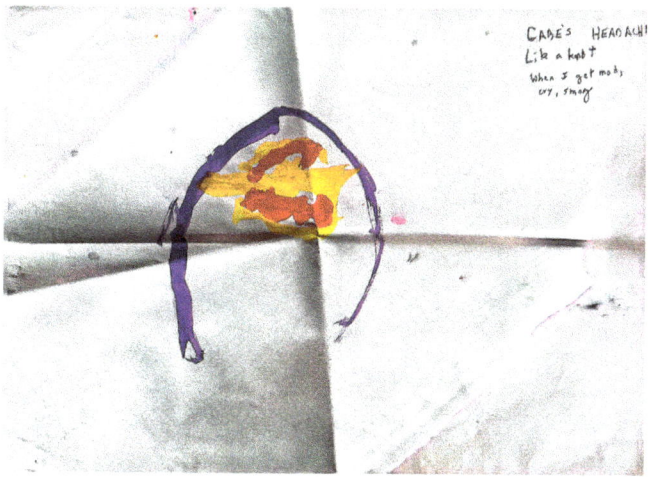

From Violet's Files

Strengthening the Sense of Self   73

Projective experiences	• How I think I look, how I wish I looked • How do others think I look • My body is amazing because, One thing I wish • Imagine your body is a rosebush
Self-nurturing process	• Identify introject around body image • Draw this part • Express anger • Find the origin • Find a self-nurturing voice for the introject
Fun, playful, and imaginative experiences with the body	• Simon sez • Dance • Pantomime • Give yourself a hug and smile because you deserve it

Recreated from Violet's Handouts

Rational For Using Movement

Contact with your body enhances the sense of self.

- Notice movements that are easy, hard, new, familiar, etc.
- Blow cotton across the table. Try this on the floor, so the whole body is involved.

Engages sensory integration: Can be a reparative experience for children who missed the experience of being on their tummies.

Violet would notice a certain movement including the ones noted below:

- How a child enters a room
- Walk into school
- A friendly body posture
- A not friendly body posture
- How does someone know you're mad, sad, glad, scared
- Show each emotion using your body

Movement can Enhance Sense of Self

- Any way you're using the body is for sense of self
- Using the polarities - walk very slowly, walk very quickly. Helps children learn about themselves.
- Imagine that you're in a play and you only have your body and face to show emotion. How do you do that?

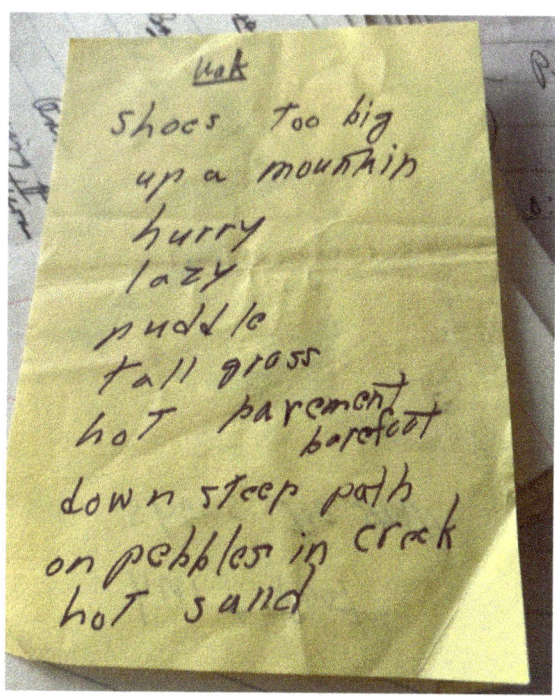
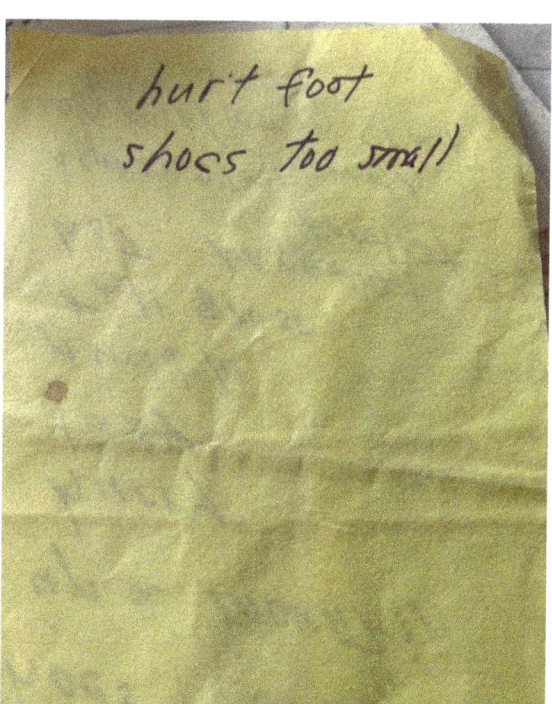

From Violet's Files

Strengthening the Sense of Self

Interventions for the Senses

Taste	• Bring in samples of things to taste and compare taste and textures
Hearing	• Making loud and soft sounds, higher and lower, with drums or other instruments
Sight	• Looking at things through glass, water, cellophane, magnifiers, kaleidoscope
Smell	• Guess that Scent Game
Touch	• Putting objects in a bag and guessing what they are by their textures
Body	• Simon sez
Breath	• Blow up balloons and keep them in the air with breath
Voice	• Sing

Recreated from Violet's Handouts

Interventions for Cognition

The Oaklander Model enables clients to be in contact with their cognition, a key contact function. You can help clients understand the connection between their emotions and their ideas by exploring how certain thoughts or beliefs elicit specific emotional reactions. This may be done through the activities below:

90 second pause:
- Name the thought(s) and feeling(s)
- Allow the uncomfortable feeling to move through your system
- Check back in "about" the initial thought and feeling(s)

Solving Problems:
- The problem: How I feel
- The solution: How I want to feel
- The process of getting there: What is the bridge?

Use polarities:
- Examine the polarity of a challenge
- Make a sandtray, a drawing, etc.

Reflect on strengths:
- What has helped me overcome challenges in the past?

Use cognition to review initial treatment goals and assess progress.

Each session, go back to the goals:
- What were our goals?
- Any additions, deletions, or changes?
- What is my progress?
    Issue:
- Where I started:
- Where I am now:
- Working with reality at the end of session:
- What can I do, think, or feel to make progress towards my goals?

Strengthening the Sense of Self

- Who can help me?

Self-Regulation

Children and adolescents, as they strengthen their sense of self, can achieve better emotional homeostasis by learning effective ways to observe, tolerate, and modulate their reactions to difficult situations. The process of depicting their feelings in itself provides some distance on them, which renders them more manageable.

From Violet's Files

Interventions for Creativity

Use fantasy	• What if _____ was possible • What would it look like, feel like, be like
Think of your best idea and your worst idea	• Reflect upon your feelings of both • Power of curiosity and questioning
Examine introjects about	• Pressure to Perform • Perfectionism • Failure

Recreated from Violet's Handouts.

Self-Nurturing Process

Violet typically initiated the self-nurturing process towards the end of therapy since addressing introjects requires the client's strengthening their sense of self. Detailed in the Key Concepts chapter, introjects are messages about themself a child receives that can result in limiting beliefs about their identity and worth. These labels can be negative (clumsy, stupid, lazy), but positive characterizations can also be harmful. The messages may also be covert rather than overt, leading to misinterpretations. Children lack maturity and cognitive capacity to reject judgments about themselves that don't fit. They take in these messages and develop a faulty belief system which derails the independent development of their sense of self. So only once their sense of self has been strengthened can they explore, assess, and integrate the power of introjects.

In fact, many adults retain these introjects. Violet explained that every one of us has some faulty beliefs about our self which lead to behaviors we reject but can't seem to change. So in some ways we are all operating on the belief system of a four- or five-year-old, as most of our self-concept was formed in early childhood. What we believed then, and how we behaved then, are in large part what we still think and do now.

From Violet's Files

By identifying the introject, such as referenced in this drawing, "you have to be perfect," helping the child express their feelings about it, and discovering its origin—the steps of the self-nurturing process—the child can find a compassionate voice within that might change how they feel and think about themself. As noted, Violet wanted children and adolescents to have strong enough boundaries to know who they really are rather than accept others' definitions of them.

The list below is taken from Violet's case notes when she asked a client to identify their negative beliefs about themself. These were then addressed during the self-nurturing process.

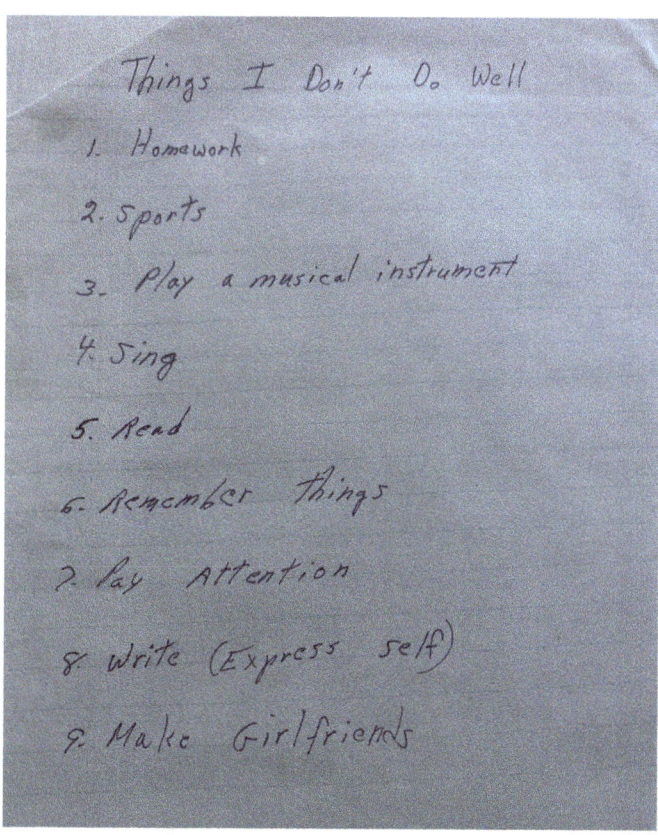

An example produced by this prompt reveals client awareness of their ideal versus their real life.

Self-Nurturing Process 83

By identifying the introject, helping the child express their feelings about it, and discovering its origin—the steps of the self-nurturing process—the child can find a compassionate voice within that might change how they feel and think about themself. The diagram shows a way for children and teens to use a rating scale to identify the level of disturbance they feel about these qualities they don't like, and conversely how strongly they feel they embody some of their positive traits.

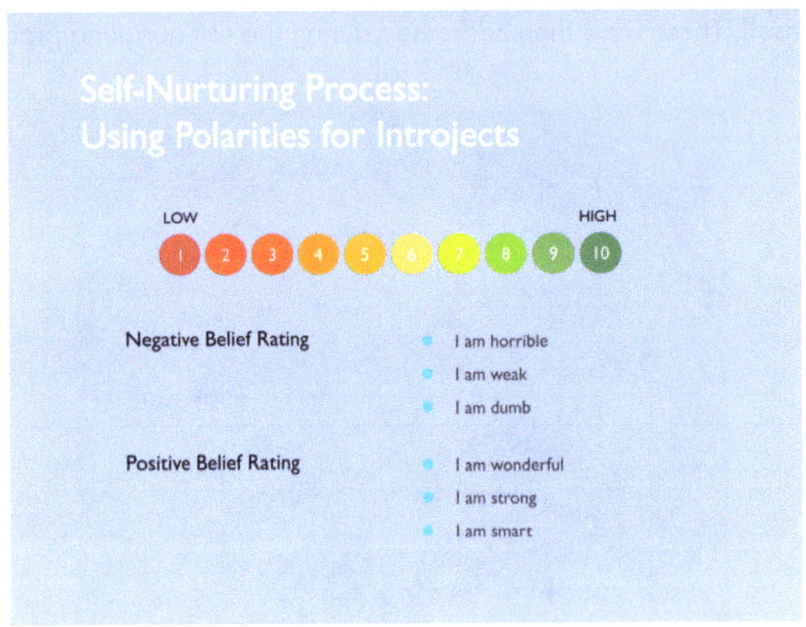

Graphic by Kathy Miu.
Copyright Healing Connections by Karen Fried.

Most of all, Violet intended for young persons to care for, and about their true self. She used a Fairy Godmother puppet to deliver this self-nurturing message to the child. We have found that the same role can be embodied by a variety of figures—even a shark puppet! In 2 separate training cohorts, 2 participants from different parts of the world identified their "fairy godmother" puppets as the shark. They both shared that a shark may be viewed as a decisive, powerful, and authentic being whose messaging one can—maybe better!—trust.

Overview: Self-Nurturing Process: How to Help Clients Acknowledge and Integrate their Introjects

The self-nurturing process comprises three phases:

Phase I: Identify the introjects or parts of themself that they don't like.

1. Talk about them.
2. Choose one part to work with.
3. Personify that hateful part.
4. Get in touch with anger at that part.
5. Explore its origin.

Phase II: Nurture the self.

1. Find the nurturing part within the self.
2. Use a Fairy Godmother or other figure supportive of the self.
3. Have the nurturing part speak to the hateful/introjected part.
4. Check in with the child.

Phase III: Practice.

1. Ask the child to find an object that represents the part to be nurtured, hugged, loved.
2. In session or at home, have the child make a list of nice things they can do for themselves.

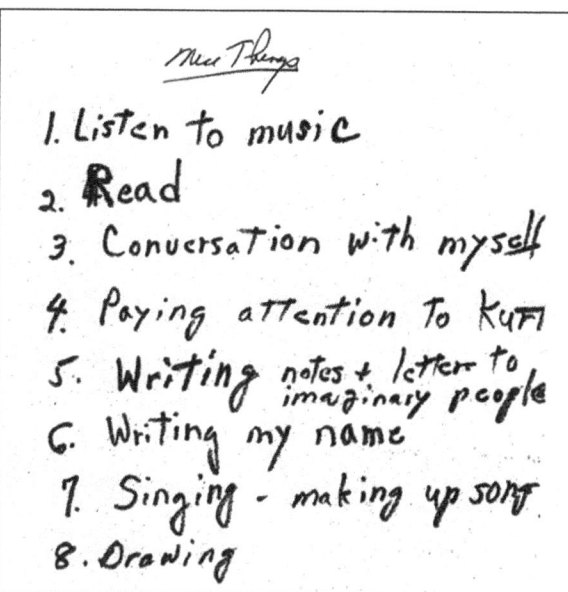

Self-Nurturing Homework from Violet's files:
List of Nice Things Client Can Do For Themself.

Parent Education and Family Work

Violet shared some guidelines for therapists about working with parents. All of these suggestions are based on the crucial I-Thou relationship:

Policies and Procedures
- Explain your policies and procedures.
- Educate parents about the therapeutic process.
- Discuss confidentiality and its limits.
- Be clear about your policies on time, fees, phone calls and other matters.
- Honor your own boundaries and limits.
- Document what you tell parents.

Establishing and Maintaining your Relationship with Parents
- Build a relationship with them.
- Emphasize the importance of working as a team.
- Remember that it is difficult to be the parent of a struggling child.
- Follow the principles of the I-Thou relationship.
- Avoid being critical or judgmental.
- Take time to tell them why "I Don't Fix Kids."
- Help them set priorities.
- Discuss how anger is expressed in the family.
- Ask how it was expressed when they were children.
- Resistant parents soften when the kids get stronger, contrary to common beliefs.
- The family does not fall apart when their children get better.
- The family system is not the only system that affects children.
- Advise parents not to pry the child regarding the session.
- Discuss confidentiality and laws in the first session.
- Help parents notice the small changes.
- Remind parents that if they need to talk to you, it should be at the beginning of the session, not the end.
- Be clear about your rules about time, fees, phone calls, etc.

During Therapy
- Never leave a child alone in the waiting room; an adolescent might be an exception.
- Set a separate appointment for parents who need to speak with you privately.

- Ask parents of very young children not to leave to go on errands during the session.
- See the child 3-5 times for evaluation. Then meet with parents/caregivers and the child to discuss the treatment process and goals.
- Advise parents not to press the child to talk about their sessions.
- Don't be afraid to be confrontative.
- Help parents notice the small changes.
- Resistant parents soften when the kids get stronger.
- Remember that the family system is not the only system that affects children.

When advising therapists as well as parents. Violet added some more technical reminders. Yet these rest equally on the foundation of an I-Thou relationship with even the youngest child:

Contact
- Be present—be in contact with yourself and your client.
- Take the child seriously.
- Be respectful.
- Join the child's rhythm and, if possible, her or his physical level.
- Observe their eyes, voice, movements.
- Repeat back what they tell you: "Johnny hit you."
- Clarify what you hear. If you don't understand, don't pretend you do.
- If you got it wrong, say so and try again.
- Use figures or puppets, or draw, or role play.
- Remember: Children always raise their voices when they want to be heard.
- Anger—angry expressions—is a child's way of expressing the SELF.

Your Communications
- Use your normal, natural voice—not a "teacher," patronizing, teasing or jovial voice.
- Pay attention to your choice of words to be sure the child understands you.
- Use sound and gestures to show you're listening. Stay present.
- Don't lecture, explain anything, or try to fix anything. Don't give advice immediately; you can talk later about what could be helpful.
- Articulate for them. Don't ask too many questions. Say, "I bet you didn't like that" or "I bet that was fun." They'll tell you if you got it right or wrong.

Violet would educate parents about how to apply the I/Thou relationship with their children. In her article:

Listening to Children: Letting Them Know You're Listening

Most children do not feel listened to. I think that's what causes so many problems. I'm reminded of a mother and 4 year old boy who came in to see me some time ago. The mother was at her wits end because the boy had numerous temper tantrums and she felt that she was losing control. Since it's so difficult for a four-year old to be involved in an adult-like conversation, I asked them both to draw a picture of what bugged them the most about the other. The mother immediately began to draw a picture of a boy lying on the floor having a temper tantrum. The boy watched her for awhile and drew his own picture of a boy having a tantrum and a mother figure standing over him. I asked the mother to tell the boy in the picture what made her mad. She said, "I don't like it when you have a tantrum. I don't know what to do." I asked the boy to talk to the mother figure. He said, "I don't like it when you stand over me yelling when I'm having a temper tantrum!" As each talked to the pictures, rather than to each other, the boy said, "You don't listen to me." It seems the mother asked him to put his toys, strewn all over, away before dinner. He was trying to tell her that some of the toys were put there by his younger brother. Somehow she didn't get his message and would raise her voice ordering him to clean up, whereupon he would lie on the floor kicking and screaming. This scenario happened many times.

From Violet's Files

From Violet's handout *Basic Points for Parents (and Therapists) about Listening to Children*: Basically kids can be pretty reasonable if they feel listened to. I remember when one of my own children would come home from school complaining about some injustice. I would want to do something to fix it–give him advice about how to handle it. I would bite my tongue and just listen and after telling me he would run out to play, the incident was apparently forgotten.

1. Being present-being in contact. Don't let your mind wander. Block out everything but your contact with your child.
2. Joining their rhythm and, if possible, their level. If the child is standing, stand. If the child is on the floor, join her. And so forth. If she is fidgety, ignore it. She is probably nervous and anxious. Stay with her.
3. Repeat back so he'll know you heard him. "Johnny hit you."
4. Clarify (if you don't understand, don't pretend you do.)
5. Use a normal, natural voice. NOT patronizing or teasing or jovial.
6. Take the child seriously.
7. Language - use words the child can understand.
8. Use sound, gesture to show you're listening. Stay present.
9. Don't lecture, explain anything, try to fix anything, give advice at that time. (You can talk about that later.)
10. Watch eyes, movement and listen to voice tones for clues as to how the child is feeling. "It seems to me that you are really mad about this."
11. Articulate for them. Don't ask too many questions. Say, "I bet…" "I bet you didn't like that" or "I bet that was fun," "I bet that made you really mad." If you're wrong, they'll tell you.
12. Use figures to act things out. Or drawings or puppets or clay figures. Or just role play–switching roles.

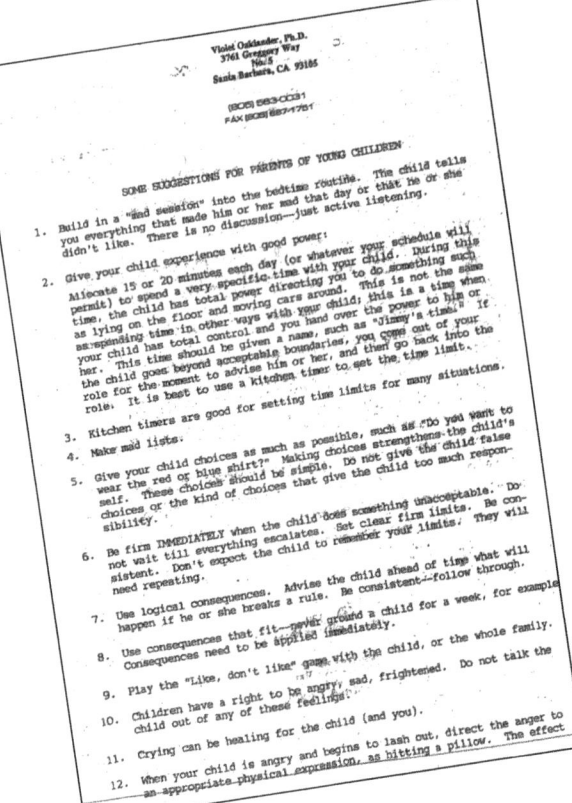
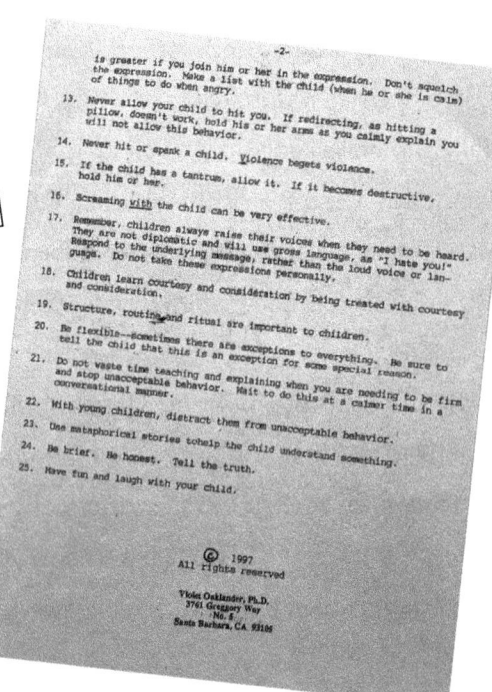

From Violet's Files

Divorce

Violet taught how divorce affects the entire family, and specified its impact on each child according to their developmental stage. She pointed out that children's reactions include a range of emotions as they deal with this transition: anger, self-blame, fear, confusion, grief and a sense of helplessness. Children are often incapable of talking about these feelings; if asked, they may respond that "Everything is fine." Yet a child might develop a variety of behaviors and symptoms indicating that all is not fine: school difficulties, acting out, nightmares, physical ailments. They may benefit from supportive adults besides parents and relatives, such as teachers and therapists.

We found these notes and drawings in Violet's file from her Divorce Workshop for therapists working with children, adolescents, and families. In it she lists the varied effects of divorce:

What Happens to the Family:

Economic changes

Changes in child care

Moving

Mother/Father as head of household

Changes in parents' mood

Anger

Depression

Anxiety

What Happens to the Children:

Usually not prepared well

Unable to express concerns and feelings

Don't believe it

Frightened

Wonder who will take care of them

Vulnerable

Fear of abandonment, especially if adopted

Denial, especially with pre-teens and young adolescents

Rejection

Loneliness

Worry about parents, especially mom, and especially if she smokes

Sleep disturbances

Somatic complaints

Depressive symptoms

Conflicted loyalties

Anger, rise in aggressive behavior

Temper tantrums

Hitting other children and siblings

Guilt, blame the self

Violet categorized these responses by age; we paraphrase her descriptions:

- 3-5: Bewilderment; sadness; fear of abandonment (separation anxiety); rise in or inhibition of aggression; guilt; disruption of pleasure in play; pursuing mastery. Regression is common: bed-wetting, clinging to security blanket; fantasizing parents getting back together; fear of replacement by another child; emotional neediness.
- 6-8: Grief; fear; feeling of deprivation; yearning for other parent; inhibition of aggression towards one or more caregivers; fantasies of responsibility for the separation/divorce and parents' reconciliation; conflicts in loyalty.
- 9-12: Denial; distress; vigorous activity and play; anger; shaken sense of identity; somatic symptoms; alignment with one parent.
- Adolescent: Worry about sex and marriage; mourning (profound sense of loss); anger, sometimes at one parent; new perceptions of parents; loyalty conflicts; sometimes greater maturity and moral growth; more realistic view of money; withdrawal from family; failure to cope; interference with adolescent developmental tasks.

Violet led the participants through an experience preparing them to work with children experiencing divorce. As seen on the next page her characteristic prompt produced powerful drawings, showing the power of this simple exercise.

- Close your eyes.
- Imagine yourself as a child hearing parents arguing and finally telling you they are separating.
- What do you feel?
- Draw something to represent the feelings or incident.

From Violet's Files

Effects of divorce leaving them feeling: "trapped, lost, dirty, blue, and sin."

From Violet's Files

Divorce Drawing: "Person in the Rain"

Working with Adolescents

Working with Adolescents

Violet was sensitive to all the developmental stages and to their lasting impact: "The old self of childhood doesn't magically disappear" in the teen years, or even in adulthood (*Hidden Treasure*, 2006, p. 97). So the earlier responses to trauma remain in effect, although mixed with concerns characteristic of adolescence. That is, their response to divorce will layer strategies of younger children with new ones elicited by their need for independence, their awakening sexuality, and their more mature grasp of others' experiences.

For example, the drive towards independence may increase adolescents' resistance to therapy, which must be honored. In *Hidden Treasure* Violet also tied resistance to another typical aspect of adolescence as a time of separating. That understanding shaped how her model manages their resistance and reaches them through authenticity and respect: "To the reluctant adolescent, I sometimes say, 'As long as you're going to be coming here to see me for a while, let's use this time to find out about yourself'" (*Windows to Our Children*, 1978, p. 292). She made her approach explicit to them: "When I work with adolescents I find that they appreciate it if I explain to them what therapy is …. They want to know how I will go about helping them find out about themselves, and what good it will do" (*Windows*, p. 294).

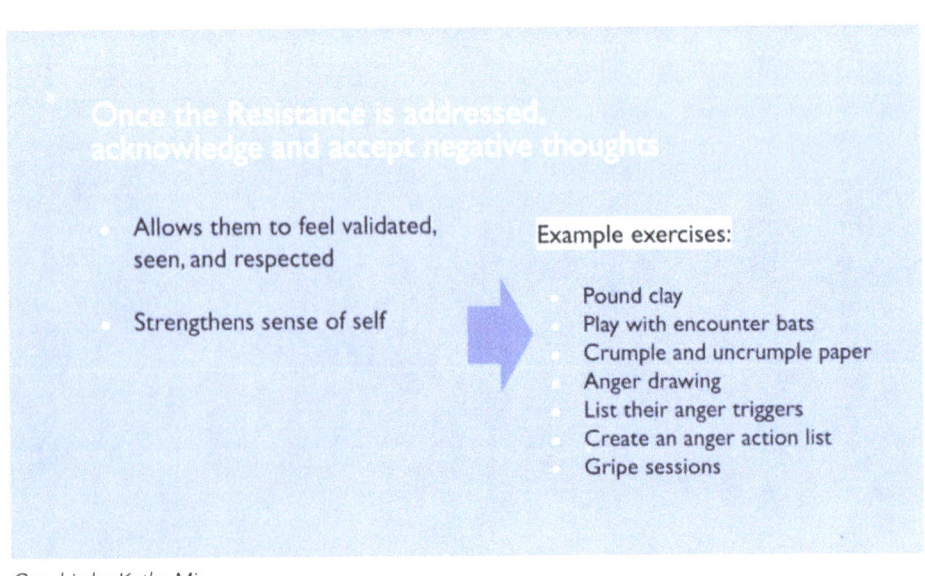

Graphic by Kathy Miu.
Copyright Healing Connections by Karen Fried.

Violet Oaklander wrote in Hidden Treasure that even when parents resist participating in therapy, therapists can still work successfully with the child or adolescent.

She emphasized that children and teens are separate individuals, even though they are of course affected by family dynamics.

In therapy, children/adolescents can:
- Learn to cope with difficulties
- Strengthen their sense of self
- Express their feelings
- Address introjects

In *Hidden Treasure*, Violet highlighted the special value of working with polarities, noting that adolescents often present one way outwardly but feel very differently internally.

When it is possible to work with the caregivers of adolescents Violet said,

"I can get a sense of the child's life, the various points of view, clarify the reason for the referral, assess the dynamics. I need to know the divergent life views—what the parents say and what the kids say, and maybe uncover what they all really mean to say" (*Hidden Treasure*, p. 98).

Play Therapy in Groups

"The group has the advantage of being a small, insulated world in which present behavior can be experienced, and new behaviors tried out. The child's way of being in the group, and how his or her behavior affects others positively or negatively, becomes clearly evident. The group becomes a safe laboratory for experimenting with new behaviors through the support and guidance of the therapist"

(Hidden Treasure, p. 175).

Often called resistance, behavioral manifestations are how the child unconsciously protects themselves. In the group, when the behavior reaches the foreground, one can examine it from all sides, play with it, exaggerate it, experience it, change it. (HT, p. 175)

Structuring Group Work
- Games with basic rules
- Art projects that are not reliant on talent, or "good" fine motor skills
- Conversation topics that are familiar to most children
- 6-8 children over the age of 8 is optimal
- 3-6 children under the age of 8
- Co-therapist is helpful
- Time limited vs. on-going
- Theme of a group – divorce, social skills…
- 1.5-2 hours duration

Plan the sessions with flexibility, to respond to the group's needs.

Begin with rounds: Each person has a turn to say something about what happened to them during the week, good or bad. Violet would take turns with her co-therapist to model rounds. Having the speaker hold a "talking stick" or other item to represent having the floor, then pass it to another group member, can be very helpful.

Chris and Karen like the group norms advocated by the Council Program (https://waysofcouncil.net/resources/):

- Speak from the heart
- Listen from the heart
- Speak spontaneously
- Speak leanly
- Confidentiality
- Whoever has the talking stick has the floor - no interrupting

Children tolerate a lot more disruption than the therapist does, so follow their cues: If the group is falling apart, stop everything and make this the theme. Therapists should adhere to their own limits and boundaries, and respect the group member's for the tone and behavior of the group.

Have an ending ritual, such as, each group member can say what they like and didn't like about the session.

Activities
- Clay
- Fingerpainting and drawing
- Puppets to encourage group interacting and to identify important persons such as friends, family members, teachers
- Playing musical "instruments" (anything that makes a sound) in a group to show feelings or tell a story.

Games
- Dreams: Share or draw a dreams
- Roles we play: The whole group can draw, act out, or choose a puppet to represent roles such as "The problem child," "The quiet one," "The funny one/clown."

Goals
- Improve social skills
- Realize that other children also have concerns. Children often believe they are the only one feeling lonely, different, isolated.
- Provide experiences to help children learn about themselves
- Appreciate that relationship is important. It can take 4-6 weeks for a group to solidify and for children to feel comfortable in it. Children are anxious and self-conscious, so early sessions should establish safety and relationship within the group.
- Strengthen contact functions, sense of self and awareness of boundary between self and others
- Express emotions, particularly anger, and understand and work through introjects
- Learn appropriate ways of behaving
- Increase mastery
- Increase contact with feelings

Facilitating these Goals
- Projective techniques: drawing, clay, music, creative dramatics, games, video, dream work, relaxation exercises, sensory exercises, body games and exercises
- Wheel to be filled in as they master each step in group participation
- Sketched outline of their body, to be filled in as they master each weekly theme

The following examples were from groups conducted by Karen Fried and Melissa Mullin at the K&M Center. Children participated in 8 weekly sessions focused on a single theme each week. After each session, every participant colored in their image of that theme, any way they wanted.

Session 1 included an interview among the participants who got into pairs, such as the interview shown here between Karen and one of the participants, as well as a "HERE AND NOW WHEEL." True to the Gestalt play therapy principles of being in the present/here and now, this worksheet invited the group members to fill in the 4 parts of the wheel with their feelings.

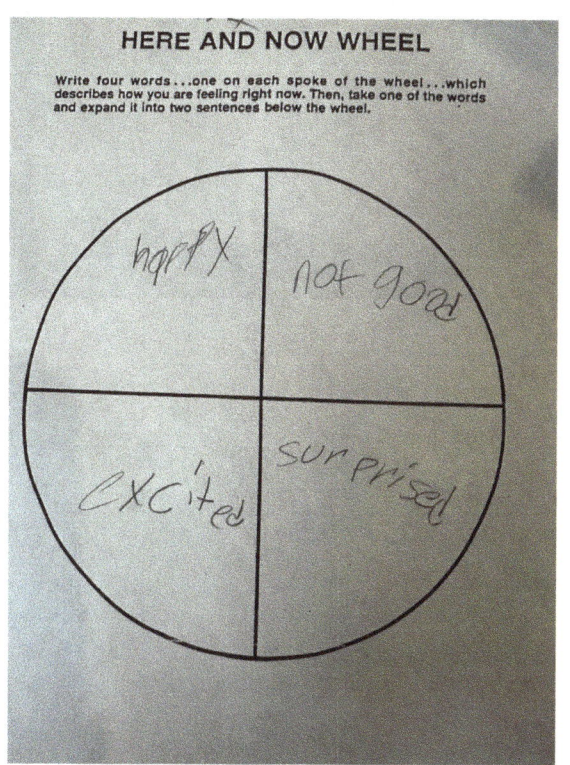 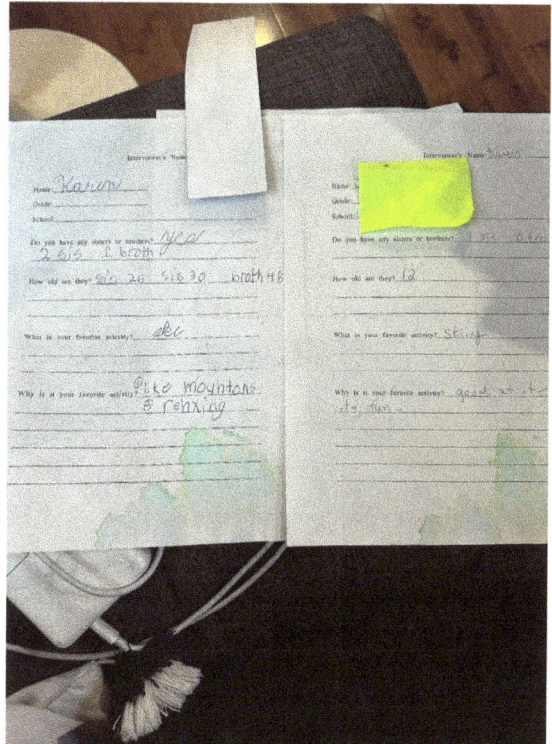

Completed Here and Now Wheels from Karen's and Melissa's Groups.

Play Therapy in Groups   105

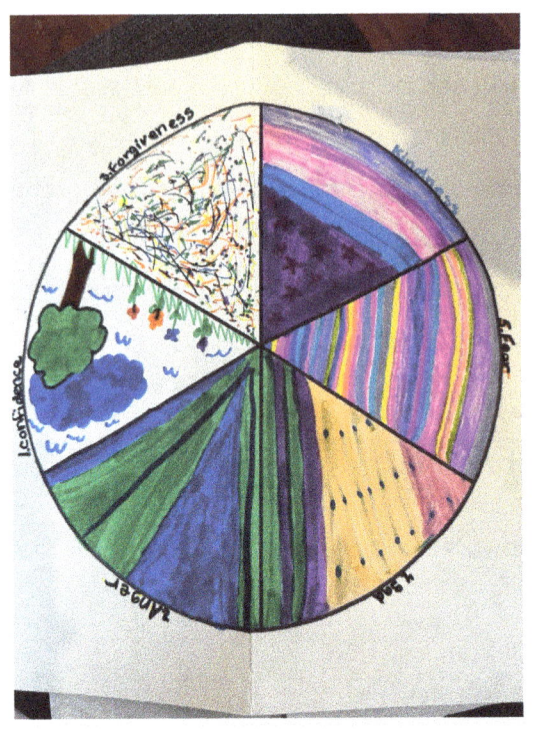
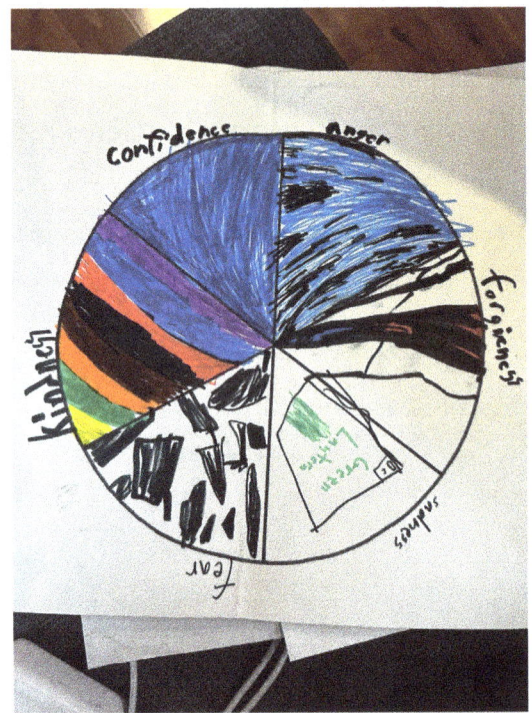

Completed Here and Now Wheels from Karen's and Melissa's Groups.

Healing Through Play - More Treasures

School Counseling

Violet often invited children to draw a picture about their experience in a given situation—including school—which provided a familiar, fun, and revealing view into the child's life. Here's a very clear expression of a child's view of what class is like for them:

From Violet's Files

From Violet's Files

This picture above (right) from her collection, drawn by a child who felt reprimanded by her teacher, is a rich response to that prompt, and one that proves the impact of school experiences on children.

Yet school-related concerns are only part of what counseling in a school setting can help resolve, key aims of her approach apply in the school context as well as in private practice: the fundamental I-Thou relationship between therapist or counselor and child; contact; honoring resistance and the child's own pace; awareness of the senses and the body; sense of self; alleviation of boundary disturbances; self-regulation; self-nurturing; awareness and acceptance of polarities; resolution of unfinished business.

Violet prompted children to dictate to her a list of what they like and hate about school. This invitation affirms their sense of self by making "I like" or "I hate" statements. Children feel heard when we allow them to express themselves, and they like lists to help organize their thoughts and feelings.

From her own career as an educator, Violet knew certain interventions work well at school, and that a teacher can and should encourage children's honest self-expression: "Teachers might not do the same in-depth work I do, but can help children make some expression—go with the fear, the feeling. Don't talk it away. Accept it. If not, children defend it!" (Oaklander notes, "How I use the media in the service of the therapy I do")

As her own career showed, all the playful and powerful exercises in the Oaklander Model are ideal for working with students in a school setting.

Preparing Yourself to Work with Children in a School

It's crucial for therapists or counselors in schools to do their own "check-in" on how they're feeling about the demands and stresses of their work. This heightens their awareness of whether and when they need resources to help them. The drawing, to the right, by an educational specialist contrasts his emotions about his role at the start of the academic year and at its close: In his words, the beginning shows a "tough climb up a hill" while, later, he's smiling on "a nice downhill."

Teacher/Ed Therapist Check-In

Your Role as a School-based Professional

The therapeutic activities you do with children in a school setting can be tailored to the school environment. This is a valuable service because children spend much of their day in school, and it can be difficult for parents to bring them to, and pay for, outside therapy. These interventions are fun and playful, and require minimal expense to implement.

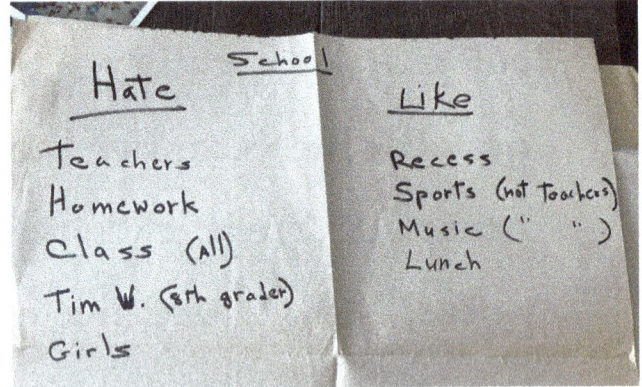
An intervention from Violet's Files: Hate/Like List

It is widely known that better academic performance is supported by better emotional well-being.

SOCIAL EMOTIONAL WORK/THERAPY:

Relevance to working in schools
- Amount of contact hours
- More than some parents
- Much more than therapists

- Facilitate mastery of what might be the most important and most measured skill set
- Reciprocal relationship between emotional well-being and successful school year
- Parents can be resistant to therapy for their kids

WORKING IN A SCHOOL SETTING: CONSTRAINTS

- Shorter sessions (e.g., 20 minutes at a time)
- May be the only counselor, child may not be able to get outside therapy
- Limited budget, options
- May not get a chance to work with the parents

WORKING IN A SCHOOL SETTING: ADVANTAGES

- Access to kids
- Know the peers
- Access to the teachers whom the children may be with more in some cases than their caregivers.

Classroom Tips to Promote Emotional Literacy and Regulation

Some classrooms have a "Calm Corner" where children can regulate themselves when needed. Yet what we learned from Violet is that children benefit from the chance to first express any aggressive energy and/or anger, or any emotion.

Adult supervision and support are helpful for safe expression of aggressive energy, anger and strong emotions.

Anger and Aggressive Energy Corner:
- Area where they can tear paper, throw clay if it's available, scribble aggressively on paper, use a pool noodle, soft battaca to hit a chair, or the floor.
- Options for movement - throwing a nerf ball into a net
- If discipline is necessary, add more recess time, rather than use as a punishment.
- Consider times when instruction can occur with the children standing and moving while learning.

Calm Corner:
- Sensory activities available, such as magnifying glasses, kaleidoscopes, musical instruments, scented markers, sensory discs that have a variety of textures to touch, snacks if appropriate to the setting,
- An eye mask they can use to rest for a set period of time.
- Headphones with soothing music if possible.
- Coloring options both structured and blank paper. etc.
- Practicing mindful strategies - using the breath

As seen, Violet advocated that school professionals use projective techniques to encourage children's self-knowledge and self-expression. These activities, described in this guidebook as noted, include:
- Projective Cards
- Drawings
- Anger/Feelings Lists
- Anger/Feelings Iceberg
- Clay/Play-Doh/Model Magic
- Batakas/Pool Noodles/Sticky Balls
- Feelings Wheel/Cards

Telehealth Treatment Using the Oaklander Model

Online child therapy—telehealth treatment—has been proven effective and beneficial even compared with traditional office visits. Its value is especially visible when using Violet's flexible projective activities and inclusive approach, captured in Karen's distance versions of the model's interventions (Fried, *Psychotherapie-Wissenschaft*, Vol. 13 No. 1 [2023], https://psychotherapie-wissenschaft.info/article/view/1664-9583-2023-1-59). Yet the telehealth mode carries unique advantages and challenges.

Setting up Telehealth Sessions

Setting up virtual sessions with online intervention apps is easy; for detailed instructions on specific distance activities, see Karen's articles at Amazon.com: The Therapist's Notebook for Systemic Teletherapy: 9781032267937: Cobb, Rebecca A.: Books). The general procedure for sessions using virtual intervention apps is the same:

1. Survey the online apps you will offer: Explore all their options and try them out yourself.

2. With parents/caregivers, set a pre-session preparatory routine tailored to virtual visits: In place of the traditional preparatory routine for in-person office visits—car or bus trip; pressing the "here" button; settling into the waiting room—discuss with caregivers how they can encourage a getting-ready routine for distance sessions, such as a snack; restroom break; and starting the computer.

3. As you would in person, offer the client a choice of activity. Then share, and have them share, screens to use the chosen activity. This lets you meet the client where they are and prioritize the self-affirming power of choosing.

4. Once your screens show the chosen activity, explore its options: The first time, have the client browse the image and functions options (described below for each app). Again, letting the client elect which exercise to do, and how to do it, supports their sense of self.

How to Use the Apps

PUPPETS

This tele-tool offers 32 puppets (images of persons, animals, and objects) and 8 backdrops; options to size and position puppets in front of or behind others; and the liberty to make them hug, hit, jump, and speak.

Instructions

Explore and Practice

Both therapist and client go to onlinepuppets.org. Once there, either can select full screen (at the bottom of the screen) for a wider view.

Ask your client to browse through the collection of puppet figures and backdrops on the right side of the screen. Have them pick a puppet figure and a backdrop and then experiment with the functions described below.

Place, Size and Orient the Figures

To place a chosen image on the backdrop, click on the figure. To enlarge or shrink a figure, drag on any of the orange handles around the figure. The top center dot around your figure allows you to rotate it toward the left or right.

Control the Puppets

At the screen's top are more buttons to enhance use of the puppets:

Use the hug button to see two figures turn towards each other and embrace.

Select speak to open your figure's mouth.

Use hit to make a figure hit another.

Use jump to see a figure jump.

Use copy to duplicate an image as many times as you want in your scene (e.g., place many children in the classroom backdrop).

By default, puppets hit and hug towards the right; use flip to reorient a puppet towards the left (e.g., to face another figure).

Your newest selected image will always appear in front of existing figures, but the back and front buttons let you reposition them.

Use delete to remove an image.

When your scene is complete, use the save button at the bottom of the screen to save it to your desktop as a .jpg, or press clear to start from scratch.

Controlling Multiple Puppets Together

Multiple puppets can be controlled together by selecting two or more puppets at once, by one of the following methods:

- Click on the stage and drag your mouse to draw a box around the puppets you wish to control together, then release the mouse button.
- Add additional puppets one at a time by holding the shift key on your keyboard and then clicking on each additional puppet.
- Click on the all button (note this will select all of the puppets on the stage).

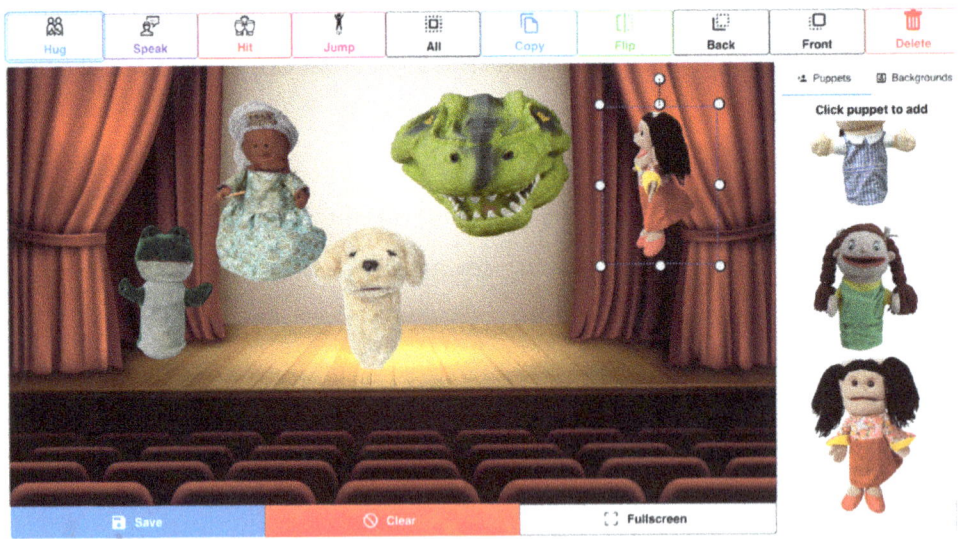

Online Puppet Show App

SAND TRAY

Instructions

To get started, both therapist and client go to onlinesandtray.com. Ask your client to browse through the collection of available figures (tabs 1-7) and explore the functionality.

Manipulating the Figures

To insert an image into the Sand Tray simply click on your desired picture. To resize an image, drag on any of the orange handles around your selection. The top center circular dot around your image allows you to rotate left and right.

Understanding Sand Tray Controls

On the top right you will find more buttons to enhance how you can use the sand tray:

Use copy to duplicate the image, you can copy as many times as you want to create your scene (e.g., place many children in a classroom in the background).

Use flip to have your figure face the other direction (e.g., to have figures talking).

Use delete to remove a single image.

You can bring images forward and back by using the back and front buttons. Your newest image selection will always begin on top of the other figures, you can use these controls to adjust.

You can press save to send the scene as a .jpg to your desktop, or press the clear button to start again.

Online Sand Tray App

Tips for Using Alongside Your Client

Once you are confident using the platform, provide your client with a prompt, and ask them to:

- Imagine a scene.
- Make their scene by clicking on each image to add it to the sand tray.
- Describe their scene to you. Use this projective exercise to ask the client to be some of their figures.
- Follow up with the question: "Does this scene make sense to you in your life?"
- Leave the scene up and open until after your client's session is over.

PROJECTIVE CARDS

Virtual or physical cards have unlimited uses, and admirably serve as projections of one's self. Each level of the projective process they're used for has value for the child, and it's not necessary to do all of them.

Instructions

Both therapist and client go to projective cards on oaklandertraining.org. To begin a session with a client, select New on the left side; this will be saved under the Themes section on the top right of your page. You can now name your exercise and include a prompt or question. You can also create as many as you want in a single session. Note, there will be an X at the top right corner when you need to close any open window.

Have your client explore the cards. You can add to the Theme/prompt whichever cards engage your client, and any number of cards, one at a time. Once your client has finished selecting cards, you can view them by selecting See all Themes.

You can work through any number of our Levels, below:

- Level 1: Pick a card and share it.

  Enhances the ability to make a choice and to make a connection by sharing that choice.

- Level 2: Share the experience of choosing a card.

  Observe their process as they choose a card. Was it fast, slow, needing help, fun, frustrating? As appropriate, encourage their increased level of connection and self-awareness as they experience or discuss their own process.

- Level 3: Describe the card in detail.

  Describe shapes, forms, colors, objects, and people on the card for greater connection and engagement.

- Level 4: Describe the scene using "I."

  Asking the client to be a part or the whole picture strengthens their capacity to project parts of themselves onto the card. This ability enhances their sense of self, creativity and imagination.

- Level 5: Questions to deepen the projection.

  Asking "What's it like to be that part?", "What do you do as that part?" allows the child to connect to a part of themselves that they may not otherwise talk about.

- Level 6: Gauging process.

  Watch for clues in voice tone, posture, expression and silence. All may signal a child's process.

- Level 7: Owning.

  Asking "Does this fit in your life?" or "Do you ever feel that way?" invites the child to gain awareness of their life as reflected in the projection. If they say, "No, it can be due to resistance, and they need to strengthen their sense of self further to own the projection. Yet they can still benefit from the experience.

- Level 8: Refocus on real life.

  Leave the scene, and explore how the awareness can be applied to the child's life.

Online Projective Cards App

DOLLHOUSE

Instructions

Both therapist and client go to onlinedollhouse.com. Ask your client to browse through the collection of available figures (tabs 1-7) and explore the functions.

Manipulating the Figures

To insert an image into the Dollhouse, click on it. To resize an image, drag on any of the orange handles around your selection. The top center circular dot around your image allows you to rotate it left or right.

Understanding Dollhouse Controls

On the top right you will find more buttons to enhance use of the Dollhouse.

Use copy to duplicate the image, you can copy as many times as you want to create your scene (e.g., to fill a room with many people).

Use flip to have your figure face the other direction (e.g., to have figures talking).

Use delete to remove a single image.

Your newest selected image will always appear in front of the other figures; press back or front buttons to reposition the figure.

When your image is complete, you can press save to keep a .jpg on your desktop, or press the clear button to start again.

Tips for Using Alongside your Client

Either ask your client if there's a scene they want to create, or provide them with a prompt and ask them to:

- Imagine a scene.
- Make their scene by clicking on each image to add it to the dollhouse.
- Describe their scene to you. Use this projective exercise to ask the client to be some of figures (people, animals, or objects).
- Follow up with the question: "Does this scene make sense to you in your life?"

Online Dollhouse App

Leave the scene up and open until after your client's session is over.

MINDFUL DRAW

Instructions

Both therapist and client go to mindfuldraw.com. You can watch the video on the left of the screen for tips, then click on the blue button.

In the top right corner you will see a settings button, which allows you to control the various functions in the app.

Select Sound to play calming music while you work. There's also an optional timer here if you'd like to do a timed practice: Click the back arrow to go back to your setting menu. On the bottom left you will see a play button, which controls your music as you work.

Select Brush Size to change the thickness of your strokes. The rate you move your cursor will also change the thickness of your lines.

Select Brush Color to explore different color options.

Select Brush Fade to change how quickly your brush strokes fade from the scene.

Select Brush Style to change your brushes' marks between free draw and blotter.

On the top right, press save to save a .jpg to your desktop, or press clear to start over.

Once your settings have been modified, click the settings button again to close the menu and begin the exercise. Simply touch and drag your cursor around the black space to draw anything you wish. You will see your strokes slowly disappear as you continue to draw.

Tips for Using Alongside your Client

Mindful Draw works because:

- There's no worry about making a mistake
- Clients know the image will fade
- It emphasizes the process rather than an end product
- It focuses on the here-and-now
- It encourages improvisation and creativity

Helpful prompts to support your client explore Mindful Draw:

- "How are you feeling right now? Close your eyes and get in touch with the feeling and make the design. Take deep breaths and watch it fade."
- "Think of something you want to let go of—what's on your mind? Close your eyes and think about whatever that is and draw that. It could be shapes, lines and even colors."
- "You can pair this app with other media that is lasting, such as a word cloud, drawing, or clay."
- "You can use it to tell a story."

Online Mindful Draw App

Telehealth Treatment

Online MindBody

The Online MindBody app allows clients to visually map out where they experience emotions in their bodies, and help them connect their thoughts, feelings and senses.

Key Features

- Body Mapping with Color and Emotion

  Clients can select from a *color palette* and make the body any color and place words or draw images *anywhere on the body image* to represent physical sensations, emotional states, or areas of stress or comfort.

  – Multiple body images can be on the screen at once (e.g., "before and after," "me at home vs. me at school").

  – Skin tone options reflect diverse identities, supporting inclusivity.

- Emotion Word Integration

  A menu of *emotion words* (e.g., "angry," "anxious," "proud," "lonely") allows users to label feelings directly on the body image to support emotional literacy.

- Taste and Sound Descriptions

  Clients can drag and drop *taste* (e.g., "sweet," "bitter," "metallic") or *sound* (e.g., "buzzing," "silence," "music") words onto the body or surrounding space to express sensory experiences tied to their emotions or environment.

- Themed Backgrounds

  Just like the Puppet App, this tool offers *background settings*—such as a bedroom, classroom, forest, or beach—to give context to what the body is experiencing and help set the emotional tone.

How to Use the App in Therapy

1. Open the App: Visit PlayTherapyApps.com and select the MindBody App.

2. Choose a Body Image: Select one or more body outlines and adjust skin tone to reflect the client's identity.

3. Add Emotion, Color, and Sensory Labels: Use the color palette to "paint" the body with feelings, then add emotion words, tastes, and sounds to describe the internal experience.

4. Select a Background: Place the figure in a setting that helps the client contextualize their inner world.

5. Reflect and Explore: The therapist can guide discussion using what the child created:
   – "What does that color feel like in your chest?"
   – "What's happening in this background that adds to the feeling?"
   – "Let's look at how these two body images are different."

Online MindBody App

Termination

From Violet's Files

When I think of saying good by I say the leves [leaves] fall

Violet outlined the meaning and process of termination specific to work with children in *Hidden Treasure* (2006). She noted that parents may resist therapy for their children because they fear treatment will be long. Yet while some children, especially those marked by significant trauma, need long-term therapy, the Oaklander Model is relatively short-term (3-6 months), since most children haven't accumulated a lot of "unfinished business."

Children might reach a plateau in their progress, and this can be a good stopping place. In fact, this plateau can let them integrate therapeutic experiences and changes within their own natural maturation. On the other hand, the plateau may signal resistance, which needs to be respected, since the child knows at some level that they cannot tolerate more therapeutic work at this time. They may need more growth, more strength. The therapist can learn to recognize the difference between an appropriate stopping place and a stumbling block worth waiting out:

Clues to Know When It's Time to Stop
- The child suddenly becomes very involved in outside activities–sports, clubs, friends—and therapy begins to get in the way of their life.
- The child no longer seems to look forward to sessions as much as they had after any initial wariness disappeared.
- The child's behavior has improved, as reported by the school and the parents.
  - Of course, behavioral improvement alone may not be reason to stop therapy. They may need more opportunity to integrate their sense-of-self work outside of the sessions.

Preparing a Child for Termination

Termination is so important that we recommend starting the therapy process with the end in mind. Included with the goals and treatment plan that are communicated to the client and caregivers is also an explanation of how the process of ending therapy is handled in the Oaklander Model.

It's also helpful to let the client know that termination need not be final—it's more like coming to a stopping place, an ending "at this time." Some children benefit from reassurance that they'll be able to come back if they need to (if, indeed, it is possible).

Providing Closure

We often overlook this important part of a therapeutic (or any) relationship. That's because saying goodbye brings up uncomfortable feelings of loss. Yet since both adults and children have many transitions in their lives, facilitating closure is a crucial skill.

Whether they are transitioning to another therapist or you are ending your treatment for any reason, plan to initiate termination a month before sessions will end:

- If the client is transitioning from your care to someone else, let them know that their therapy can continue.
    - Discuss their ongoing treatment goals with them.
- Talk about the reasons for termination. If you're the one ending the therapy, explain why you're leaving (job change, move). Explanation is important because children are egocentric and might take the blame—or the credit—for your departure.
- Together, do an overview of their work with you, and specifically detail progress they made from the start to the present.
    - Termination in private practice or in schools can include a picture or other creation the child can keep, made in their choice of media, colors, lines and shapes, showing "what it feels like now to be leaving this office (or classroom)."
    - You may respond to the created work by noting that we always have some unfinished business about separation and goodbyes. There's nothing wrong with being sad (or glad!) over endings.
- Encourage them to talk about the positive and negative aspects of your work together. Let them know it's safe to say what they didn't like or what they wish could have been different.

Hidden Treasures

Hidden Treasures

We're so happy that we can share all these resources that we found in Violet's many files. These prompts invite clients to express themselves in any medium, including drawing, sand tray, puppets, collage, paper, clay, writing, and performances. And therapists get the same freedom: Even when directing specific interventions, you'll respond to your client's process and result to encourage their self-expression and self-awareness. So this chapter illustrates projective experiences as examples of tools you can adapt for your clients.

Prompts - these prompts were from a handout Violet provided in the notebook we all got at her two-week training in Santa Barbara:

1. Take a fantasy trip (through the woods/ up a mountain/ into a cave/ through a door).
   Step into your place.
2. Visualize your world in colors/ lines/ shapes/ symbols or any combination.
3. Do some breathing exercises, and make a scene about:
    – what you do when you're angry
    – how you would like to be
    – what makes you angry
    – a scary place
    – something scary
    – the last time you cried
    – a place that makes you happy
    – how you feel right now
4. Go back to a memory and make a scene of:
    – a time you felt the most energy
    – a family scene
5. Imagine an ideal place:
    – where you wish you could be
    – a favorite place you've been
6. Imagine, and show, a favorite time.
7. Recall the worst thing you can think about.

8. Look at this picture (any picture) or listen to this (any sound) for two minutes. Now draw/ make something that shows how you felt while looking/ listening.

9. Think of, and show, your family:
    – now
    – in the past
    – in symbols
    – as animals
    – as dabs of color
    – as the family you wish you had

10. Imagine yourself, and show:
    – the part of you that you like best
    – the part of you that you like least
    – your outer self
    – your inner self
    – how you see yourself
    – how others see you
    – how you wish others would see you

11. Think of, and show:
    – a person you like/ hate/ admire/ are jealous of

12. Think of, and show:
    – your monster
    – your demon

13. Imagine, and show, how you get attention.

14. Think of, and show, what you do when you feel:
    – depressed
    – sad
    – hurt
    – jealous
    – lonely, a time you felt lonely

15. Show an imaginary animal.

16. Show something that annoys you about:

    – someone here

    – someone close to you

    – yourself

    – the world around you

17. Make a scene to represent a time (or times) in your life:

    – your day

    – your week

    – you as a child or younger child

    – you as a teen

    – you as an adult

    – when you were happy/ loving/ sad/ angry/ scared

18. Make sounds with any drawing you've done.

19. Use body movements with any drawing you've done.

20. Have a family, pair, or group make a scene:

    – with each member adding something

    – with all deciding on a theme and making the scene together

    (Observe their process and interaction.)

21. Use your dominant hand, then your non-dominant hand, to draw a picture of:

    – a point in childhood

    – a dream

    – part of a story/ fantasy/ poem

22. Imagine, then show, your polarities:

    – weak/strong

    – happy/sad

    – what you like/don't like

23. Imagine, then show, a physical pain:

    – headache

    – stomachache

    – cut

24. Do a Scribble about:

    – being laughed at

    – being bullied

    – mastering a task

25. Think about, then show:

    – your most pressing problem

    – a roadmap of your life

    – your favorite dinner

26. Think about, then show, images of yourself:

    – where I am now in my life

    – where I come from

    – where I used to be

    – where I want to go

    – what's keeping me from getting there (blocks/ obstacles)

    – what I need to get there (resources/ supportive people/ inner qualities)

27. Listen to, then fill in, this sentence:

    – I used to be _____ but now I'm _____.

28. Have the client lie on a large piece of paper, and use a marker to outline them. Then have them ask themselves how they felt:

    – yesterday

    – this morning

    – now

    – how you will feel tomorrow

    – how you feel being selfish/ stupid/ crazy/ ugly/ mean/ serious/ silly

29. Imagine, then show:

    – a secret

    – something you want

30. Draw or paint to music:

    – something you need

    – three wishes

    – being alone

    – being with others

31. Take a crayon or marker and just allow your hand to move over the paper and do whatever it wants to.

32. Listen to these words, and draw quickly to represent them:

    – love

    – hate

    – beauty

    – anxiety

    – freedom

    – charity

33. Draw yourself as an animal, and place yourself in a setting.

34. Let's tell a story together. (Violet used collaborative storytelling techniques as projective devices that deepen exercises, including sand tray, puppets, creating games, making up or changing fairy tales, drawing, clay and use of all media. If the client agrees, the stories may be recorded; you may later examine them as part of the Child Apperception Test.)

Clay Self-Sculpture:

Clay Self Sculpture from Karen's Online Training

We found this experience in Violet's notes on a notecard, scribbled in her handwriting. This activity may be done by a single client, group, or family:

- Make a round ball of clay. As you do, become friends with your clay. (Wait a few minutes.)
- Now, close your eyes and imagine that round ball of clay changing form into some image of YOU. It could be a real you, a part of you, all of you, or something that represents you or makes you think of you. In your mind, watch this clay change into this "you." (Wait a few minutes.)
- Now, still with your eyes closed, reach out for the clay ball, pick it up, and hold it gently. Know you're holding you. Notice how you feel. Do you feel tender toward you? Angry? Impatient? Sad? Loving?
- With your eyes still closed, form your image of you. Notice how you feel as you change yourself into your image. Let your fingers shape your image. Just let it happen. (Wait three minutes.)
- OK; now open your eyes. Look at you. (Wait a moment.) Describe this you as the clay you you've made and in first person—I, me, and my. If I ask, "How do you feel?" the clay image you would say, "I feel…." So now, how do you feel? (Let the client answer; should be in first person as the self-sculpture). What do you do? (Let them answer; they should begin, "I….") How is your life? (Let them answer; should use "My life….") What are you like? (Let them answer; should use "I'm like….")
- (If working with a family or group, have each member answer your questions in the first person as their own self-sculpture. Then ask, "Now, is there anything about anyone else's clay that is similar to you? Different than you? What do their self-sculptures say to you?") (If working with one client, ask, "Does what you made out of clay fit for you? Is there anything you would like to change about what you made?" If so, give them a few minutes to change the self-sculpture.)

Unsafe Place Drawing:

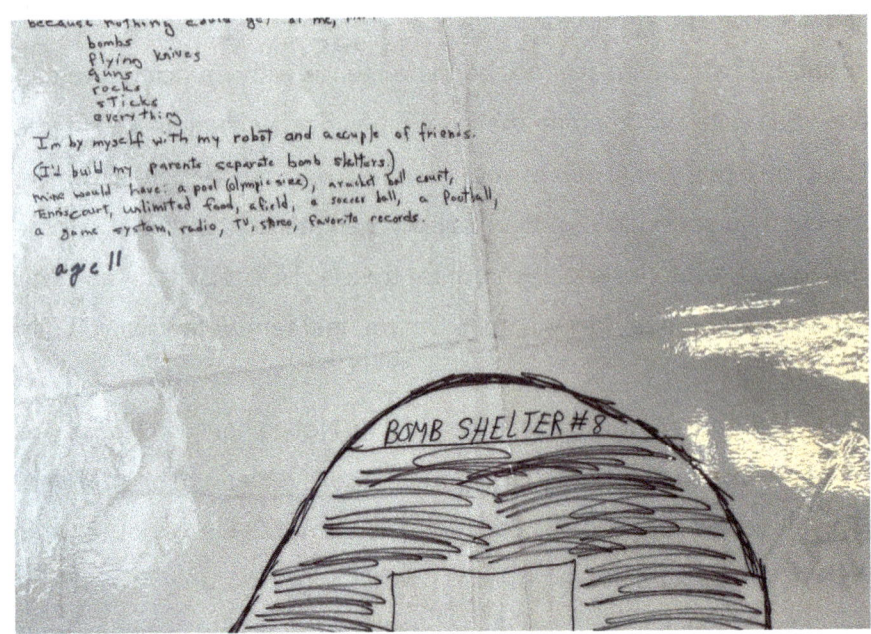

Safe Place Drawing from Violet's Files

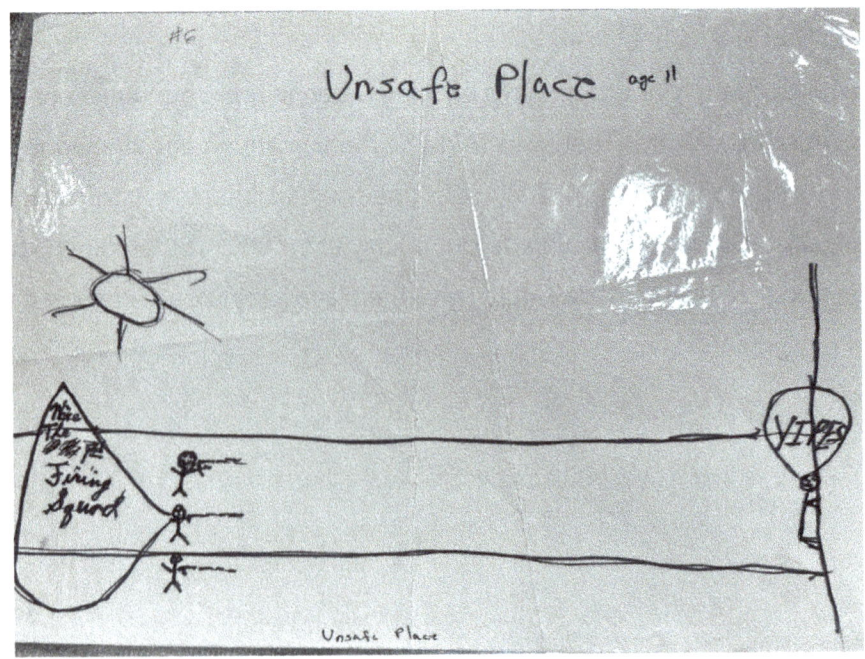

Unsafe Place Drawing from Violet's files

Violet recommended inviting clients to draw a safe place. Yet many children who have experienced trauma have lost the sense of safety which would let them confront their blocked emotions, reclaim disowned parts of themselves, and experiment with more appropriate behaviors to get their needs met.

In *Hidden Treasure* (2006) Violet noted that a traumatized child may find it difficult or even impossible to think of and depict a safe place; "You will notice their resistance, and/or they will tell you." So you may encourage them first to think of and depict an *unsafe* place. Your choice to offer that option rests on the I-Thou relationship you've built by being where the client is.

- How about (drawing/ making a sand tray scene/ picking a card about) a place that is not safe?
- Imagine what that would (look like/ feel like) for you. Whenever you're ready, make that scene.
- Once it's made, ask the client to
    - describe it
    - then to be some of its parts
    - then to talk with or as the parts
- To give them the chance to own the projection, ask if this fits for them.
- Often, having their feelings of unsafety seen and heard enables them to think of and depict a safe place.

Nemesis

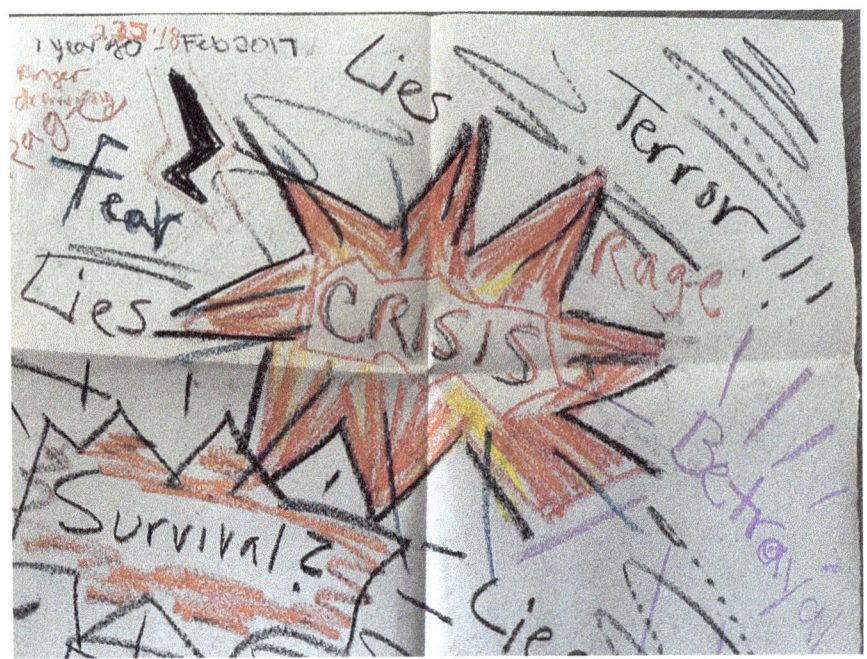

Chris's Anger Drawing

Chris's Online Kinsugi Vase

Chris generously shares her anger drawing and also work she did with Karen's new Kinsugi app. She started with a vase provided in the app, then clicks on the hammer that breaks the vase, put it back together, and painted it with gold paint as a way of healing this broken part, acknowledging the new found beauty and strength healing brings.

This activity serves when working with anger and strong emotions.

- Choose one of your drawings you'd like to go deeper into with your (anger/other strong emotion).
- Tell me about your drawing and about the (angry/other) feeling.
- Imagine the (angry/other) feeling.
- Make the (angry/other) feeling out of clay (/draw it/make an another medium).
- Be the (angry/other) feeling:
  – You can talk back and forth between the (angry/other) feeling and yourself.
  – (Based on your and your client's I-Thou relationship, the clear limits you've set, and your spirit of fun and playful exaggeration, invite your client:) Decide how you'd like to express your (angry/other) feelings—maybe by yelling, smashing and tearing paper, poking the couch with pillows, stomping. (Allow the client to do what they chose.)
- (To help the client own this object that represented their feelings, ask:) Does it fit in your life? Would you change anything in it?

Tree Movement Activity inspired by Seema Omar

(Drawing used with permission from a wonderful online participant of one of Karen's cohorts)

Invite the client to stand up if they wish. Invite them to close their eyes, if they're comfortable doing so.

- Have them take a deep breath, and as they breathe out, imagine they're breathing out from the edge of their body—from their fingers and toes and skin—kind of out through the aura surrounding their body. Then have them imagine they're a tree.
- Have them think about what sort of tree they are: tall or short; thick or thin; with dense branches or just a few. What sort of roots do they have? And trunk? Branches? Leaves? Fruit?
- Ask where they are. Ask if they like being there.
- Now, have them think about the different feelings they carry inside: happiness, sadness, anger and fear. Have them think about their trunk … and branches … and leaves .. and flowers .. and fruits. What emotions do they notice inside?
- Ask what they see around them, and what emotions does this bring up inside them. And as the wind blows through them, how do they feel?
- Suggest that there may be birds on and around them. Ask how they feel about them: Do they like them?
- Ask what happens when it rains . . . when there is a storm. . . . Do they feel afraid? Where do they feel this fear? In their trunk? Or roots? Or branches? Or leaves or fruits?
- And now, invite them back to the awareness of their breath; invite them to open their eyes if closed, and to take a few minutes to draw their tree. Remind them this drawing does not have to be perfect or beautiful or even look exactly like it is in their imagination: However it turns out is just fine.
- (On Zoom, you may ask participants to draw their tree and surrounding details in a group drawing on the whiteboard to create a forest.)

Forest Prompt:

When working with groups, Seema Omar would do a follow up to the individual trees and have group members add their trees to a forest composed of the whole group.

From Karen's Online Training

Boat in the Storm:

From Violet's Files

From Violet's Files

From Violet's Files

Along with a drawing by one of her clients, Violet's notes give us her view on the value of the intervention: "There are many ways to use the fantasy. The most effective way for me is merely to ask the child (after a meditative-breathing exercise) to imagine, with eyes closed, that he is a small boat in a big storm. I say something about the waves and the wind and the struggle. I ask the child to be the boat, to be aware of how he feels as this boat, what's happening now, what happens next. Then I will ask him to draw a picture of himself as this boat in a storm. Much material invariably comes forth about this child's place in his world and how he copes with outside forces."

- Write a story about a small boat in a big storm. The wind is wild, and the waves knock about the small boat.
- Try to imagine that you are the small boat and explain how you feel. Use comparisons in your story to tell how it feels to BE a small boat in a big storm.
- The wind shrieks and whines as it tries to sink the tiny boat. The boat fights back. Think of some kind of struggle in the animal world that is like the boat-storm situation. Write it down. Describe why this animal struggle is like the boat-storm situation.
- Imagine that you are the tiny boat. Tell what the different parts of your body must do to fight the storm.
- How do the different parts of your body tell you whether you are winning or losing the fight?
- Suddenly the wind makes one last attack on the little boat; then the wind dies. The boat has won! What real-life experiences have you had that are like the wind dying and the little boat winning the fight?
- Imagine that you are the little boat who has just beaten the storm. How do you feel toward the storm?
- Imagine that you are the great storm who can't even sink a tiny boat. How do you feel toward the boat?

Bibliotherapy

Offer your client the chance to pick a book you'll both read and talk about together.

Here, we used *Everybody Needs a Rock* by Byrd Baylor. Recall that many books for young people feature a special object you'll find useful to have; for this book, gather a small selection of rocks to keep in your office; you may also ask the client to bring a few rocks from home.

- Read the book with the child or adolescent, or invite the adolescent to read it aloud in session.
- Ask the client to choose a rock, and pick a rock for yourself. You may choose them from your selection of rocks in your office or those the client brought from home, or go outside together and choose some rocks.
- Invite the client to introduce themselves as that rock: "I am this rock...." If they have any resistance, model this by introducing yourself as a rock.
- End this experience by asking them if they might "own" the way they introduced themselves as the rock: Did it fit for them in their life? They may say, "No," which is fine: For many children, the experience of choosing the rock and projecting themselves onto the rock is more important than conscious awareness.

Haiku: Prompt and Follow-Ups

> **HAIKU FOR CHILDREN**
>
> I have used a simplified haiku-like form with children. A haiku generally has three lines of five, seven and five syllables each. I have used a simplified five-line form consisting of one word, then two words that say something about the first word, then three words that say something further, and the fifth line repeating the first word.
>
> Here are some samples:
>
> Boys
> Stupid brats
> Fight with girls
> Ugly faces, ugly hair
> Boys
>
> (9-year-old girl)
>
> School
> Run away
> Beat up someone
> Don't like to read
> School
>
> (8-year-old boy)
>
> Dinosaurs
> I wish
> They were alive
> I'd rather ride their backs
>
> (7-year-old boy)
>
> I usually write the haiku down as the child dictates to me, and read it back with dramatic emphasis.

Shared with permission by Ricardo Escobar, from Mexico, a wonderful participant who also is an expert trainer in the Oaklander Model.

For this exercise, have paper, a pencil, and a choice of instruments for each participant—individual or group members.

Ask them if they've heard of Haiku. If needed, explain briefly that it's a Japanese form of short poems that follow a pattern of syllables (or, "word sounds")—different numbers of them for different lines of the poem. Ask if they'd like to try one style of Haiku. If so, explain the Haiku style you'll be using.

- The poem has five lines. The first line has 1 syllable; the second has 2, the third has 3, the fourth has 4, and the last, fifth line, has 1 syllable, like the first line does.
- Take a Haiku walk to look at scenery (outside, if possible) for about 3 minutes.
- Give each participant a sheet of paper and a pencil. Without signing their name, have each participant write Haikus for 5-10 minutes, as age-appropriate. You will write one also.
- (If a group, gather and mix them up, and pass them around to the group; if you and one client, exchange poems. Give each participant a choice of instrument.)
- Each person reads one of the Haiku as others make music with instruments.
- Talk about the experience:
- What senses did it use (all senses, body)? What else was involved (awareness, patience)?

How did it feel (creative, relaxing, meditative, mindful, expressive)?

Knot Poem: Prompt and Follow-Ups

From Windows to Our Children pg. 99:

The poem "There Is A Knot" in *Have You Seen a Comet?* Never fails to bring forth some feelings usually kept hidden. This is a translation of a poem by an 8-year-old Turkish child:

Chris's Knot Poem Drawing

There is a knot inside of me
A knot which cannot be untied
Strong
It hurts
As if they have put a stone
Inside of me

I always remember the old days
Playing at our summer home
Going to grandmother
Staying at grandmother's

I want those days to return
Perhaps the knot will be untied
When they return
But there is a knot inside of me
So strong
And it hurts
As if it is a stone inside of me (p. 32)

The Knot Poem helps clients through the grief process. Here's just one way to use this projective exercise:

- Have the child close their eyes, if they want to; it's OK if they want to keep them open.
- Read this poem aloud to them.
- Invite them to do choose a projective exercise (picking a card, drawing a picture, or any other exercise). This will help then process their response to hearing the poem.
- If appropriate, ask them what they felt when they listened to the poem.
- If appropriate, invite them to write their own poem.

Tent Fantasy

From Karen's Online Training

This playful projective experience uses fantasy, imagination, gross motor skills and contact with body movement.

- I would like you to stand up. Stretch your hands above your head and make yourself as tall as you can.
- Notice how high the tips of your fingers are, and notice your body all the way down to your feet.
- Feel your feet press against the earth. Notice how you feel in your body. Do you have any aches or pains? Just notice. Notice your breath. (Wait a moment.)
- Now I want you to close your eyes if you're comfortable doing that. And I want you to imagine you're standing in front of a large tent with a long zipper from the bottom to the top that's keeping it closed. I would like you to take the zipper and pull it from the top a-l-l-l-l the way to the bottom.
- After you pull down the zipper, you notice the two flaps of the tent open on each side. Now I want you to step inside the tent. Notice what is now around you. What do you see? What kind of objects are in there? (Wait a moment.)
- What about sounds—can you hear anything? Are there any unique smells? How about tastes? (Wait a moment.)
- Now I want you to notice one object, or one sense, or one feeling. What is it? I want you to take that object or sense or feeling with you, and step back outside the tent. Reach to the bottom and zip the tent a-l-l-l-l the way back up. Now come back to the room, and draw that object or sense or feeling. (Wait a moment.)

Paper Experience: Prompt and Follow-Ups

Seema Omar's Paper Experience

Though brief, this projective exercise encompass working with the senses, expressing and releasing aggressive energy, and self-soothing that can support self-regulation. Choose paper that does not have toxic dyes or glitter.

- Ask the client to pick a piece of paper they don't mind smashing or stomping on. (This step increases contact with the senses.)
- Hold the paper in one hand, and fan yourself with the paper. Feel the breeze it makes. Notice how the paper feels in your hand. Put the paper up to your nose and see if it has a smell. Maybe you want to put a corner in your mouth or just quickly on your tongue. Notice the taste! (This step allows contact the senses.)
- Then think of something that's bothering you. It could be something that's slightly annoying or really makes you mad. (Wait a moment.) Start to smash your paper into a ball. Notice if you feel like putting more pressure on the paper. (This action increases contact with aggressive energy and other emotions.)
- Now that you have a smashed ball of paper, try throwing it on the ground, or maybe throw it at the wall. Once it falls to the ground, try stomping on the paper as many times as you feel like. (Wait a few moments.) Notice if you feel you got rid of some of your annoyed or angry feelings, compared to how you felt when you started. (This action encourages self-soothing and self-regulation.)
- Now, pick up your paper and notice the side that got stomped on. Feel that crumpled side; you can even hold it up to your face and notice how that feels. Then smooth out your paper with your hands as much as you can. Feel the creases with your hands. Notice how it feels to smooth out the paper after smashing it, throwing it, and stomping on it. (Wait a moment.)
- Notice how the crumpled paper looks now. You can then get a pen or marker and trace the creases in the now-crumpled paper. (Wait a few moments.)
- Look at the lines you drew, and see if you notice a design or a picture you can make out of them.
- (Ask the client,) Now be that design or picture, or part of it. (This step helps clients own the projective experience.) How does that feel to you?

Pawn Shop:

Pawn Shop Drawing: "I am a special carved wooden box with unknown treasures inside of me"
From Violet's Files

The pawn shop drawing projective experience lets clients use their imagination, incorporates past and present time frames, and engages them in a spirit of playfulness—all key components of the Oaklander Model. It follows her fundamental steps for the projective process:

1. **Imagine it:** Imagine you're in a time machine and go back in time.
2. **Make it:** Draw your experience any way you'd like.
3. **Be it:** Be one part of this drawing (and maybe other parts, perhaps in dialogue).
4. **Own it:** Apply this to your life.

- I'd like you to sit back and get as comfortable as you can. Close your eyes if you feel comfortable doing so. If you don't, just have your eyes gaze softly somewhere in front of you. (Wait a moment.)
- Let's take some deep breaths together. Inhaling in. Exhaling out. (Do this three times).
- Now, I'd like you to take your attention inside yourself and let's do a brief body scan. Let's start at the top of your head. Do you sense anything there? Tightness? Temperature? Coolness? Warmth? Nothing? If you sense tension anywhere, you can move anytime you'd like.

- Now, let's go down to your face. What do you sense there? How are your cheeks feeling? The area around your eyes? And your jaw? Do you sense any tension there?
- As we move down to your chest, notice what you sense there. And your belly and back.
- Now, down to your thighs and hamstrings, down to your knees. How about the back of your knees? We don't often think about this area. Moving your attention all the way down to your feet, I'd like you to wiggle your toes. Sometimes we forget that we go all the way down to our toes.
- Now I'd like you to listen to this (instrument you have) for as long as you can hear it. (Ring three times.)
- I'd like you to imagine that you are entering a time machine. Opening it up, you step inside and close the door. On the dashboard display you see that it's transporting you back to the year 1603. Arriving there in an instant, you open the door and step outside onto a cobblestone street. You peer up the street and see many small shops with wooden signs advertising their businesses. At the end of the street you see a small sign with the words, Pawn Shop, and you decide to go there.
- Once there, you turn the squeaky brass door knob and step inside. The shop is packed full with all sorts of items both large and small. A white-bearded old man behind the glass counter, who must be the shop owner, tells you, "Go ahead and take anything you'd like." (Wait a moment.)
- You look around and find just the right item, tell the shop owner "thank you" and "good-bye," and head back to the time machine. You get back in, and travel back to our time. (Wait a moment.)
- Let's take a big breath together and exhale. When you are ready, open your eyes or blink, and show in some way—in a picture, colors, lines, shapes, or curves—the item you chose. (Wait a minute or two.)

Closure Experience with a Window

From Karen's Online Training

This visualization may be done with an individual or with a family or group that has worked together. For each participant, print the window template below, make your own, or have them make their own. You will also need a small gong, bell, chime, or singing bowl.

- We're going to do an experience now to help you remember what we accomplished in our sessions together, and see what stands out to you. So go ahead and close your eyes, if you're comfortable doing so. Take a deep breath and let it out. Maybe when you do that you make some sound—that's OK!
- Take another deep breath, let it out, and scan your body from your head to your toes. Notice if you're feeling any pressure or tension anywhere. Just notice. (Wait a moment.)
- Now, listen to this sound for as long as you can hear it. (Ring the instrument you have two or three times, pausing in between rings.)
- Now I want you to imagine that you are inside looking out a window onto a very large meadow. In this meadow is a view of everything we have done together in our sessions. What do you see in the meadow that shows when you first came into this room (or online) with me? What did you notice then? What did you think then? (Wait a moment.)
- Remember when we did (mention a few experiences, conversations, progress updates, difficulties). As you think about these things we did or said in our sessions, maybe one thing stands out for you, or maybe many things.
- When you notice one or more things, I'm going to ask you to (do a drawing, make a sand tray scene, pick projective cards or other action they choose) and make a scene of what's in this meadow, outside the window. As always, whatever you make doesn't have to make sense, it's just for you to show what stands out to you about our work.

A screen shot (left) shows the powerful possibilities of this exercise.

Fantasy Script: "The Mouse and the Animal at the Door"

(Note: It can be any kind of animal — real, make-believe, big, small.)
Drawing used with permission from one of Chris's clients

"Let's get comfortable — maybe close your eyes if you want, or just look softly down.

I want you to imagine that you are walking along a quiet path. It's a beautiful day, and you feel calm and safe.

As you walk, you notice something moving near your feet. It's a little mouse! A very special little mouse.

This mouse is wearing a tiny hat — and when it sees you, it stops, stands up on its little hind legs, and tips its hat to you, like a little gentleman or lady.

Take a moment to look at this mouse. What does it look like? What color is it? What kind of hat is it wearing?

The mouse seems like it wants to say something to you. Maybe it does. Maybe it just smiles.

After a moment, the mouse scurries away, and you continue walking.

Now you come to a house — your house. It's just the way you would like it to be. You walk up to the front door.

And as you get closer, you see that an animal is standing at the door, waiting for you.

The animal looks at you.

Take a good look. What kind of animal is it? What color is it? How big is it?

Does it say something to you? Or maybe it just shows you something with its eyes or body?

How do you feel seeing this animal waiting for you?

What would you like to do next? You can stay with the animal as long as you want."

(Pause quietly for a while, then gently say:)

"When you're ready, you can slowly bring yourself back to the room, and open your eyes when you feel ready.

Later, if you like, you can draw or tell me about your mouse or your animal."

Polarities

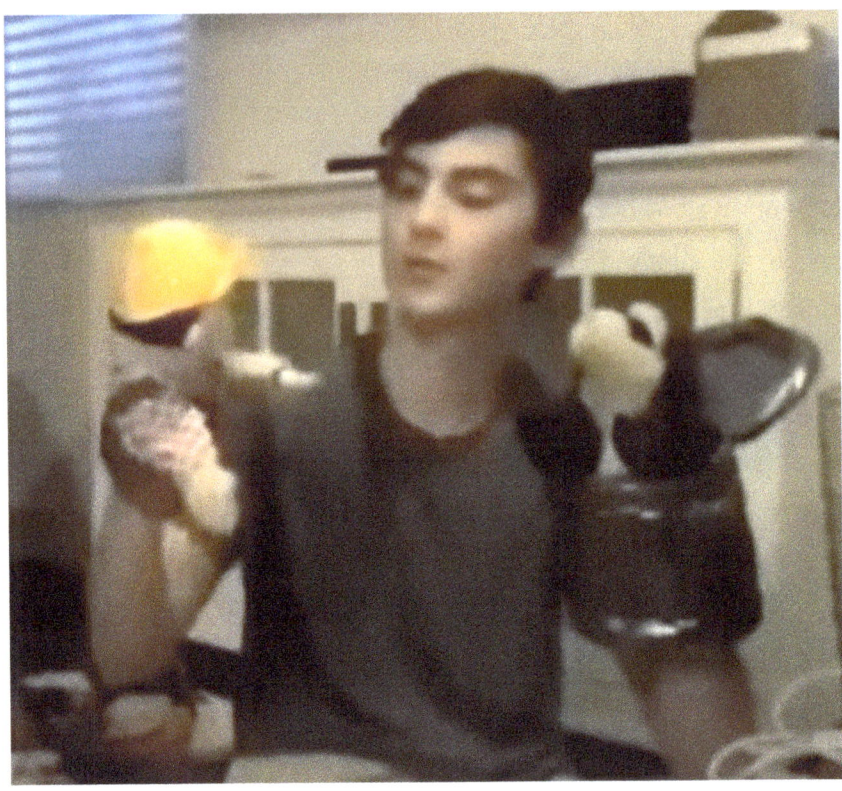

Demonstration by Karen's Teenage Son

Weak/Strong	Found/Lost
Alone/Together	Serious/Silly
Happy/Sad	Smart/Dumb
Open/Closed	Aggressive/Passive
Inner/Outer	Sane/Crazy
Brave/Afraid	Superior/Inferior
Good/Bad	Love/Hate

The Weak/Strong experience she detailed helps clients become aware of, and accept, their polarities. To do the experience, each client needs a piece of paper and pens, crayons, or markers.

Weak/Strong: Prompt and Follow-Ups

- These are ways to think about being weak and strong, and ways to draw these feelings. Close your eyes, if you are comfortable doing that. Think about what it feels like to be weak. (Wait a moment.) Now think about how it feels to be strong. (Wait a moment.)
- Now think about what it looks like to be weak, and what it looks like to be strong. (Wait a few moments.)
  - What colors come to mind? What shapes? Will you be dark, light, bright? Will you be drawn heavy? Will you fill the whole page, or part? Will you use curves, lines, angles, circles, squares, large or small shapes?
  - Don't think of real things unless you must. Be aware of your feelings now.
- With eyes open and without talking, draw your weak side on one side of the paper, and your strong side on the other. Be aware of your experience as you do this. (Wait a few moments.)
- Describe your feelings and awareness as you drew. (Give them time to speak.)
- Describe your picture as if it were you, by saying: "I am…." (Give them time to speak. Then you may comment, focusing on polarities, body language, specific parts of the drawing to increase the client's awareness of themselves).

More Treasures

More Treasures

Taken from Violet's notes and materials for her Self Workshop, and from "Experiences to strengthen the self" in our Sense of Self folder, these additional exercises are for your information and enjoyment.

Using the Senses and the Body

- Touching:
    - brush, back massager, water spritzer, Kush ball, clay, Rock Book, fingerpaint; Touch and Match Game, little pillows

Therapist has put objects in a bag and client reaches in and guesses what they are.

Describing the feel of various textures

Listing words that describe some touch sensation (bumpy, fluffy, slippery, hard, soft, smooth, sticky, gooey, warm, cold, hot, freezing, rough, holey, prickly, tingly, feathery, rubbery, thin, spongy, mushy, silky, hairy)

- Listening:
    - weird noise thing, gloom sticks, small pebble-filled bottles to shake, Sound Safari, drums and other instruments, ocean drum, music

Meditating on whatever sounds come into awareness

Painting while listening to music (fingerpainting is especially good)

Making loud and soft sounds, higher and lower sounds, with percussion instruments

Matching sounds

Having a "conversation" with just sounds, no words

Sound-recognition game

Comparing sounds with feelings

- Seeing:
    - kaleidoscope, Where's Waldo, magnifier, coloring book, No Peeking game, I Spy

Looking at very detailed pictures

Drawing, painting, or sketching flowers, fruit, trees

Experimenting with touch with eyes closed and then with eyes open: What's different?

Looking at objects through glass, water, cellophane, magnifiers, kaleidoscope

- Smelling:

Scented crayons and markers, Guess that Scent Game

Talk about favorite and not-so-favorite smells.

Pantomime smells of various things for the other person to guess.

Provide experiences with various kinds of smells (e.g., flowers, fruit, grass, sweet, spicy)

Place items with distinctive aromas in opaque containers (e.g., perfume, mustard, banana, apple, onion) and ask the client to guess the smell.

Talk about memories evoked by specific smells (or draw pictures of them).

- Tasting:

Mindfulness Orange Exercise

Discuss favorite and not-so-favorite tastes.

Bring in samples of things to taste, and compare tastes and textures.

Pantomime eating various foods.

- Breath:
    - balloons, harmonica

Experiment with different ways to breathe, and how breath affects the body.

Blow up balloons and keep them in the air with breath.

Play the harmonica.

- Voice:

Experiment with voice sounds together with percussion instruments.

Sing!

Role-play a simple sentence in various voices (e.g., pleading, angry, fearful)

Have a screaming contest.

- Body:

Twister, batakas, Kids On Stage (creative dramatics)

Fall onto pillows in creative ways.

Pantomime various games and sports.

Have a bataka fight as various characters (e.g., king and queen, two very old people, two babies).

Throw soft balls in various ways.

Play with a very large ball.

Exaggerate various movements.

Show all the movements you can make with various parts of your body.

Dance to various types of music.

Show how you can exercise sitting down.

Pantomime situations using different parts of the body, starting with fingers, then hands, then arms, and so on,

Using Reflection and Self-Expression

- Reading:

It's My Body, Everybody Poops, Peter Alsop songbook, Relaxation Meditation

Self-Statements: Projective Exercises

Projective toy exercise, projective tests, puppets, medicine cards, color test, Ungame, TFD Game, metaphors

- Aggressive Energy:

Puppets, batakas, Whack Attack, Splat, clay, dart guns, Velcro guns, clay tools (e.g., mallet)

- Discovering and Strengthening the Self

Self-Statements/Defining the Self/Owing Projections

Linda Goodman's Sun Signs

The Kid's Book of Questions

Making lists: (e.g., favorite things, likes, dislikes, wants, needs, people that make you angry).

- Focus on polarities: who I am and who I am not—using drawings, puppets, creative dramatics, clay, happy/sad, weak/strong.

Make an image of yourself out of clay—realistic or abstract.

Throw a ball and make a self-statement with each throw.

Give projective tests and find out what fits and doesn't fit according to the client.

- Do the projective toy experience.

Play games for stating an idea, thought, opinion, feeling, such as the Ungame, and the Talking, Feeling, Doing Game.

- Use metaphorical stories and folk tales. Make up the stories or use books.
- Make up puppet shows.

These suggested experiences, meant to strengthen contact functions with the body and to exercise creativity, come from Violet's notes. She directed the therapist to write each action on a slip of paper, place them in a bowl, and have the client reach in, pick one, and act one it out. The exercises cover contact with each part of the body.

- With the fingers:

Typing

Playing the piano

Sewing

Cutting wrapping paper

- With the hands:

Catching a fly, holding it, then letting it go

Kneading dough

Punching air

Washing yourself

Cutting paper

Holding taffy or sticky glue

Catching a ball

- With the arms:

Sawing wood

Rocking a baby

Swinging a bat

Swimming

Rowing

- With the hips:

Using a dust mop

Wiggling like a bunny

Hula dancing

Using a Hula Hoop

- Feeling your body:

Feel toes, mouth, tongue, chin

Weight

Heavy

Light

Cement shoes

Hands are balloons

Fat

Skinny

Arms are feathers

Body is very dull

You are …

- In a tiny box

- In a big box

- A chicken in an egg: How would you get out?

- Letting your arms lead

- Using every part of your body:

Windshield wiper

Tree in wind

Swinging a bat

Cowboy's walk

On a Ferris wheel

- Walk:

Happy

Tired

Big and strong

Afraid

Fat and jolly

Angry

Sneaky

Shy

With soap in eyes

Carrying lighted candle, for using imagination

On slippery ice

At a parade

Up a hill

Down a hill

Long steps

Stiff legs

- Be an animal:

Butterfly

Cat

Chick

Dog

Duck

Elephant

Frog

Grasshopper

Horse

Kangaroo

Rabbit

Snake

Squirrel

Ostrich

Monkey

Crocodile

Giraffe

- Pretend you're a:

Witch

Elf

Cowboy

Ghost

Circle

Square

Letters

Giant

Clown

Crooked lane

Triangle

Curve

Games:

Violet further identified games addressing specific therapeutic issues and Lynn Stadler presented this at a JFN session:

- Establishing the I-Thou Relationship:
    - Ungame, Book of Questions/Talking Feeling Doing Game
- Allowing Appropriate Power and Control:
    - Any game where the child is appropriately in charge (e.g., the child can choose the role you take in a creative dramatics experience; they can decide on the game that is played when the parents/siblings/family members in a session).
- Body/Breath/Movement/Awareness:
    - Tag, Charades, Twister, Kids on Stage, any pantomime game, sitting on a large ball, throwing soft balls, batakas, Operation
- Releasing Aggressive Energy Safely:
    - Splat, Whack-a-Mole, Don't Break the Ice, Nerf games
- Sensory Awareness:
    - I Spy, Guess that Smell, Matching Sounds, Simon Says
- Managing Anxiety:
    - Jenga, Don't Break the Ice, Pick-Up-Sticks
- Transition, Integration and Grounding:
    - Uno, Connect Four, Candyland, Chutes and Ladders, Hangman, Trouble, Mancala, card games, Tic-Tac-Toe

EMOTIONS LIST - THINGS THAT MAKE ME...

What are some things that make you feel each emotion? List them below.

HAPPY	SAD
ANGRY	WORRIED
PROUD	CALM

Graphic by Kathy Miu. Copyright Healing Connections by Karen Fried.

We close this second guidebook after having reviewed every file Violet left us when she passed in September of 2021. We included much of what we found and are honored to share it with you.

Both of these guidebooks have been our labor of love to continue her legacy. We are grateful for having had this opportunity, and for your interest in Violet's work.

Karen and Chris

www.ingramcontent.com/pod-product-compliance
Lightning Source LLC
Chambersburg PA
CBHW080518030426
42337CB00023B/4564